The Law of Article V

State Initiation of Constitutional Amendments

Robert G. Natelson

THE LAW OF ARTICLE V: STATE ORIGINATION OF
CONSTITUTIONAL AMENDMENTS
©2018 by Robert G. Natelson
All rights reserved

Published by Apis Books, Golden, Colorado, 2018.
Printed in the United States of America.

Without limiting the rights under copyright reserved above, no part of this publication may be reproduced, stored in or introduced into a retrieval system, or transmitted, in any form, or by any means (electronic, mechanical, photocopying, recording, or otherwise), without the prior written permission of the copyright owner.

Interior and exterior book designs by D.J. Natelson and Apis Books.

About the Author

Robert G. Natelson is the nation's most published active scholar on the U.S. Constitution's amendment procedure. After approximately a decade in the general practice of law, he embarked on an academic career. Over the succeeding 25 years, he served as a law professor at three different universities, teaching and writing in a wide range of legal fields, among them constitutional law, advanced constitutional law, First Amendment, constitutional history, remedies, real property law, and fiduciary law. He has authored or co-authored legal treatises for some of the leading legal publishers in the English-speaking world.

Professor Natelson is best known as a constitutional scholar, and his meticulous historical and legal publications have covered most of the Constitution. In addition to his work on the amendment process, he has published groundbreaking research on the Constitution's Necessary and Proper Clause, Postal Clause, Elections Clause, Coinage Clause, Commerce Clause, and other provisions. His scholarship has been cited repeatedly by justices of the U.S. Supreme Court, by federal appeals court judges, and by the highest courts of at least fifteen states.

Among Professor Natelson's more recent books are *The Original Constitution: What It Actually Said and Meant* (Apis Books, 3rd ed., 2014) and *The Origins of the Necessary and Proper Clause* (Cambridge Univ. Press, 2010) (with Lawson, Miller, and Seidman).

He is currently Senior Fellow in Constitutional Jurisprudence at the Independence Institute in Denver, where he heads the Article V Information Center.

Preface

The United States Constitution prescribes the methods for amending itself. Article V of the Constitution informs us that all amendments must be ratified by legislatures or conventions in three fourths of the states—but that before amendments can be ratified, they must be duly proposed.

The Constitution provides for two modes of proposal: by Congress and by a temporary gathering the Constitution calls a "Convention for proposing Amendments." Congress must call a convention for proposing amendments on "the Application of the Legislatures of two thirds of the several States."

Some contend that not much is known about the application and convention procedure because the Constitution provides little detail. Of course, the Constitution also provides little or no detail about many other institutions and procedures it references: trial by jury, the writ of habeas corpus, bills of attainder, ex post facto laws, and so forth. We know all about them, nevertheless, because we have studied the history, law, and practices of those who wrote and adopted the Constitution.

Before 2010, I was among the many who harbored erroneous assumptions about the application and convention procedure. During a research project, however, I was able to correct those assumptions by consulting the same kind of sources that clarify the meaning of other constitutional terms. These sources include Founding-Era law and political practices, writings and speeches delivered at the time, and a great many Founding-Era official documents.

Yet the sources for understanding the application and convention procedure do not end with the Founding Era. They include three centuries of interstate and inter-colonial convention practice, over two centuries of post-Founding official documents, hundreds of state legislative applications, and a string of court decisions stretching from 1798 into the twenty-first century.

This treatise explains the principles and rules governing Article V's application and convention procedure. It consists of four Parts. Part I lists the major writings on Article V and classifies them into three groups or "waves," according to chronology and accuracy, and it alerts the reader as to which writings are generally reliable and which are not. Part II is a Table of Cases cited in this treatise. Part III provides extensively documented exegesis on the application and convention procedure. Part IV is a collection of forms.

I hope you find this material interesting and useful.

Robert G. Natelson
Denver, Colorado
November 19, 2018

Table of Contents

About the Author i
Preface iii
Part I. Sources, "Science Fiction," and Article V Bibliography 1
   § 1.1. Sources 1
   § 1.2. The Loss of Knowledge 4
   § 1.3. Reliability of Modern Article V Bibliography 5
   § 1.4. Major Publications 8
Part II. Table of Cases 13
Part III. Explanatory Text with Footnotes 17
   § 3.1. Historical Background 17
   § 3.2. Types of Conventions 21
      § 3.2.1. In-State and Multi-State Conventions 22
      § 3.2.2. Proposing and Ratifying Conventions 22
      § 3.2.3. Plenipotentiary and Limited Conventions 23
      § 3.2.4. Categorizing the Constitutional Convention and the Convention for Proposing Amendments 24
   § 3.3. Why the Founders Adopted the Proposal Convention in Article V. 26
   § 3.4. Analyzing the Text of Article V 29
   § 3.5. Applicable Legal Principles: Interpretation, Incidental Powers, and Fiduciary Obligations 32
   § 3.6. Assemblies Acting under Article V Do So Solely by Virtue of Powers Granted by Article V. 35
   § 3.7. Under Article V, a State "Legislature" Means the State's Representative Assembly, without Participation by the Governor or by Any Reserved Power of Initiative or Referendum. 39
   § 3.8. The State Legislatures' Applications 43
      § 3.8.1. Background 43
      § 3.8.2. What Is an Application and How Is It Adopted? 44

§ 3.8.3. *State Legislatures May Limit Their Applications to a Single Subject.* 46
§ 3.8.4. *Application Format, Conditions, and Subject Matter* 48
§ 3.8.5. *State Legislatures May Rescind Applications.* 49
§ 3.8.6. *Unrescinded Applications Do Not Grow "Stale" with the Passage of Time.* 50
§ 3.9. The Congressional Role in Calling the Convention 52
§ 3.9.1. *The Meaning of "Call".* 52
§ 3.9.2. *Contents of the Call* 53
§ 3.9.3. *Congressional Powers Incidental to the Call* 56
§ 3.9.4. *The Necessary and Proper Clause Does Not Authorize Congress to Structure the Convention.* 58
§ 3.9.5. *If Thirty-Four Applications on the Same Subject Are Received, the Call Is Mandatory.* 62
§ 3.9.6. *Counting Applications* 64
§ 3.10. Selecting Commissioners 72
§ 3.11. Empowering Commissioners 73
§ 3.12. Instructing and Supervising Commissioners 74
§ 3.13. "No Runaway" Acts and Similar Laws 74
§ 3.14. Convention Rules 75
§ 3.14.1. *The Legal Environment* 75
§ 3.14.2. *Historical Resources* 78
§ 3.14.3. *Formalities before Adoption of Rules* 81
§ 3.14.4. *Recommended Rules Not Pertaining to Debate or Decorum* 87
§ 3.14.5. *Rules of Debate and Decorum* 97

Part IV. Forms 105
§ 4.1. Citizens for Self-Governance Form Application 105
§ 4.2. Sample Form Electing Commissioners 106
§ 4.3. Sample Commissions 107
§ 4.4. Sample Instructions 109
§ 4.5. The Uniform Interstate Convention Act 112
§ 4.6. Historic Examples of Multi-State Convention Calls 118
§ 4.7. Model Convention Rules 122

The Law of Article V

State Initiation of
Constitutional Amendments

Part I.
Sources, "Science Fiction," and Article V Bibliography

§ 1.1. Sources

Many sources offer insight into the meaning of Article V. The first resort is, of course, the constitutional text. However, as is true of other questions of constitutional law, the meaning of the text of Article V is not always self-evident. In such instances, the courts typically rely on Founding-Era or other historical evidence of meaning.[1]

Founding-Era evidence for interpreting Article V is largely of the same kind used for interpreting other parts of the Constitution: word definitions and usage in eighteenth century dictionaries and other contemporaneous sources; the records left by the Constitution's framers; the ratification debates in the state conventions and in public venues (such as newspapers); state legislative material from the Founding Era; the proceedings of the First Federal Congress; and eighteenth century law and legal documents. Uniquely important for interpreting Article V are state legislative resolutions and applications adopted when the Constitution was being debated and the records of the many previous "conventions of states" for which the convention for proposing amendments was the model.[2]

---

[1] *See infra* § 3.5.

[2] Robert G. Natelson, *Founding-Era Conventions and the Meaning of the Constitution's "Convention for Proposing Amendments,"* 65 FLA. L. REV. 615 (2013) [hereinafter Natelson, *Conventions*]. Since publication of that article, another convention of colonies has been identified. It was held in

There is also a very rich store of post-Founding evidence. Approximately fifty court cases cast light on the procedure.[3] Moreover, hundreds of state legislative applications have been adopted since the Founding.[4] The years 1899 through 1912 witnessed an application campaign for direct election of U.S. Senators, which resulted in at least 29 states passing applications.[5] At that point, Congress rendered further proceedings unnecessary by formally proposing the Seventeenth Amendment. Similarly, the 1940s witnessed a campaign for a convention to recommend limiting the President to two terms,[6] after which Congress proposed the Twenty-Second Amendment. During the 1960s, thirty-three states applied for a convention to partially reverse Supreme Court decisions requiring all state legislative chambers to be apportioned solely by population.[7] Beginning in the 1970s,

---

Albany, New York in 1684. *See The 37th "Convention of States" Discovered,* http://articlevinfocenter.com/the-37th-convention-of-states-discovered/. However, the total number of conventions of states and colonies is now known to be higher than 37. For an updated list, see *List of Conventions of States and Colonies in American History,* http://articlevinfocenter.com/list-conventions-states-colonies-american-history/.

[3] *See infra* Part II.

[4] Applications are collected at *The Article V Library,* http://article5library.org/ (last visited Oct. 4, 2018), and one may undertake subject searches there.

[5] *Article V Convention Application Analysis,* THE ARTICLE V LIBRARY, http://article5library.org/analyze.php (filter by "Direct election of Senators") (last visited Oct. 4, 2014).

[6] *Id.* (screen by "Limit Presidential Tenure").

[7] This campaign died out partly as a result of the passing of its leader, Senator Everett Dirksen (R-IL) and partly because liberal opponents disseminated claims that an Article V convention was a "con-con" of uncertain composition that might "run away." Although such claims were not original, this seems to have been the first application campaign in which they had a significant political impact. *See* ROBERT G. NATELSON, THE LIBERAL ESTABLISHMENT'S DISINFORMATION CAMPAIGN AGAINST ARTICLE V (2015), available at https://www.i2i.org/wp-content/uploads/2015/01/Campaign-v.-Article-V-final.pdf.

states have applied regularly for a convention to propose a balanced budget amendment.[8]

A third source of post-Founding evidence is comprised of the records from the first-ever ratification of a constitutional amendment (the Twenty-First) by state ratifying conventions rather than by state legislatures. Before Congress chose the convention method of ratification in February, 1933, some alarmists predicted that state conventions might fail or even veer out of control. Nothing of the kind happened: The states adopted protocols for the election and convening of delegates, and the procedure was completed successfully in less than ten months.[9]

A convention for proposing amendments is a gathering traditionally called a "convention of the states" or "convention of states."[10] The protocols applying to such meetings, both before and after the Founding, tell us much about how a convention for proposing amendments will work. There have been more than forty gatherings of this type, the first a convention of colonies in Albany, New York in 1677 and the latest a convention of states in Phoenix, Arizona in 2017.[11] In addition, in 2016, the Convention of States project of Citi-

---

The applications for a reapportionment amendment differed so significantly that it might have been impossible to aggregate all thirty-three. *See Article V Convention Application Analysis*, THE ARTICLE V LIBRARY, http://article5library.org/analyze.php (filter by "Apportionment") (last visited October 4, 2018). The same cannot be said of the applications for direct election of Senators. *See id.* (filter by "Direct election of Senators").

[8] At one time thirty-two of the necessary thirty-four states had applications for a balanced budget convention in force. *See Article V Convention Application Analysis*, THE ARTICLE V LIBRARY, http://article5library.org/analyze.php (filter by "Balanced budget") (last visited October 4, 2018).

[9] *See generally* EVERETT SOMERVILLE BROWN, RATIFICATION OF THE TWENTY-FIRST AMENDMENT TO THE CONSTITUTION OF THE UNITED STATES (1938).

[10] *Infra* § 3.2.4.

[11] JOURNAL OF THE BALANCED BUDGET PLANNING CONVENTION, PHOENIX, ARIZONA, SEPTEMBER 12, 2017 – SEPTEMBER 15, 2017, *available*

zens for Self-Governance held a simulated convention in Williamsburg, Virginia. It included commissioners (mostly state legislators) from every state.[12] Several conventions of states (most notably the Washington Conference Convention of 1861) drafted and recommended constitutional amendments.

Clearly, there is no lack of material for guidance on Article V procedures.

§ 1.2. The Loss of Knowledge

If an American Founder such as John Dickinson or Alexander Hamilton were to visit us today, he would be astonished at how little most Americans—even those working in constitutional law—know about the application and convention procedure of Article V. To the Founders, interstate convention protocols were familiar and well-understood, and they fully expected the application and convention process to be employed.

As public understanding of the convention process faded during the twentieth century, it was replaced with a great deal of misinformation. Claims about the convention procedure were characterized by empty speculation, groundless alarmism, and very little investigation.[13]

---

at http://articlevinfocenter.com/wp-content/uploads/2018/10/BBA-Journal.pdf [hereinafter JOURNAL].

[12] *Convention of States, Historic Simulation*, at https://conventionofstates.com/cos-simulation.

[13] For a survey of the opponents' disinformation campaign, *see* ROBERT G. NATELSON, THE LIBERAL ESTABLISHMENT'S DISINFORMATION CAMPAIGN AGAINST ARTICLE V (2015), http://articlevinfocenter.com/wp-content/uploads/2018/10/Disinformation.pdf, and HOW THE NEW YORK TIMES AND THE WASHINGTON POST SPREAD "FAKE NEWS" ABOUT AN AMENDMENTS CONVENTION (2016), http://articlevinfocenter.com/wp-content/uploads/2018/10/Natelson-NYT-WP-Art-V.pdf.

§ 1.3. Reliability of Modern Article V Bibliography

One way we can understand the relative value of modern Article V writings is to classify them into three phases or "waves":

- *First Wave* publications date mostly from the 1960s, 1970s, and early 1980s. These were authored predominantly by liberal academics who opposed conservative efforts to trigger a convention and who therefore emphasized uncertainties.

- *Second Wave* publications were issued between 1979 and 2000. The Second Wave was a transitional body of work relying on additional sources. Virtually no scholarship on the subject was published between 2001 and 2010, so . . .

- *Third Wave* publications are those written since 2010. In the aggregate, they fully reconstruct convention procedures and law from all the historical and legal sources.

First Wave publications tended to be agenda-driven. Even when they were not, they were the product of little serious research and many false assumptions. For example, virtually all First Wave authors assumed that the only relevant precedent was the 1787 Constitutional Convention, and none—not even the law professors among them—seemed aware that the Supreme Court had characterized an amendments convention as a convention of the states.[14]

In the absence of reliable facts, First Wave authors created a largely speculative version of Article V. Of course, speculation in the absence of facts is always risky, and sometimes produces comical results. Before scientists were able to penetrate the clouds covering the planet Venus, science fiction authors posited a land of jungle and swamps—a vision obviously unconnected to the truth.[15] In like manner, First Wave writers portrayed an amendments convention as an

---

[14] Smith v. Union Bank, 30 U.S. 518, 528 (1831).

[15] *See The Greenhouse in the Sky?*, CHEMISTRY WORLD, http://www.rsc.org/chemistryworld/Issues/2006/April/GreenhouseSky.asp (last visited Oct. 10, 2018) (contrasting prior science-fiction speculation with the actual surface of Venus).

untethered, congressionally sponsored "constitutional convention" dominated by a mob of placard-wavers. One writer compared it to the Republican and Democratic National Conventions, in which hordes of passionate and popularly elected delegates become flushed with the power to remake the country.[16] Somewhat inconsistently, other First Wave authors argued that Congress could exercise tight control over the assembly by reason of its power to call it. Most First Wave authors were unaware of the history of judicial involvement in Article V issues, and therefore thought the courts could have little role in constraining the process.

First Wave speculations were encouraged by ignorance of Founding-Era practices and vocabulary. For example, some authors asserted that because the Founders had referred to an amendments convention as a "general convention," the gathering was necessarily plenary or unlimited as to subject. They did not understand that the Founders' term "general" referred to the number of states participating, not the scope of the agenda.[17]

The "science fiction" version of Article V largely dominated commentary during the 1960s, 1970s, and into the early 1980s. Although its bizarre portrayal of an amendments convention has been thoroughly discredited, it continues to be promoted by some lobbying groups today.

Dissatisfaction with raw speculation encouraged a new breed of writers to revisit the issue. The beginning of the Second Wave can be

---

[16] *E.g.*, Phyllis Schlafly, *Is Article V in Our Future?*, TOWN HALL MAG., Aug. 27, 2013, *available at* http://townhall.com/columnists/phyllisschlafly/2013/08/27/is-article-v-in-our-future-n1673875/page/full. ("Now imagine Democratic and Republican conventions meeting in the same hall and trying to agree on constitutional changes.").

[17] Natelson, *Conventions, supra* note 2. For examples of this misunderstanding, see Charles L. Black, *Amending the Constitution: A Letter to a Congressman*, 82 YALE L.J. 189, 198 (1972) (describing an unlimited convention as a "general" one), and Walter E. Dellinger, *The Recurring Question of the "Limited" Constitutional Convention*, 88 YALE L.J. 1623, 1632 n.47 (1978–1979) (assuming that because Madison referred to a "general" convention, he meant an unlimited one).

dated to 1979, when John Harmon, a Justice Department lawyer, produced an extraordinary legal opinion for the Department that actually relied on some Founding-Era evidence.[18] The most elaborate Second Wave publication was Russell Caplan's book, *Constitutional Brinksmanship*, released in 1988 by Oxford University Press. Caplan utilized ratification materials and court opinions in his study, and even made brief reference to earlier interstate conventions.

Access to this wider range of sources led most Second Wave authors to conclude that an Article V gathering could be limited as to subject. But their unfamiliarity with other aspects of the record induced them to persevere in some First Wave errors. For example, several continued to refer to an Article V conclave as a "constitutional convention," and some assumed that Congress had authority to prescribe the method of delegate selection. Some even committed new mistakes.[19]

The Third Wave of publications began around 2010. Third Wave findings enlist not only the records of the Constitution's drafting and ratification, but also the pre-existing convention tradition and contemporaneous law. These materials are supplemented by court decisions and actual practice over the centuries since the Founding. As a result, Third Wave writings have relegated earlier commentaries to merely historical interest.

Following are the principal conclusions of Third Wave scholarship:

---

[18] John M. Harmon, *Constitutional Convention: Limitation of Power to Propose Amendments to the Constitution*, 3 OP. O.L.C. 390 (1979).

[19] Thus, in Bruce M. Van Sickle & Lynn M. Boughey, *A Lawful and Peaceful Revolution, Article V and Congress' Present Duty to Call a Convention for Proposing Amendments*, 14 HAMLINE L. REV. 1, 28–29 (1990–1991), the authors argued that because the word "Amendments" in "Convention for proposing Amendments" was in the plural, it was unconstitutional to limit the convention to a single subject! This conclusion not only flies in the face of common sense, but of history as well.

- A convention for proposing amendments is a diplomatic meeting among delegations representing the state legislatures—that is, a convention of the states.

- It is a limited-purpose gathering, not a "constitutional convention."

- It was modeled after a long tradition of limited-purpose multi-state assemblies that followed established protocols and procedures.

- Not only can the convention be limited as to subject, but Founders expected all or most amendments conventions to be so limited.

- Congressional power over the convention process is restricted to counting and classifying applications and setting a time and place for meeting.

- Article V questions can, and often have been, adjudicated by the courts.

§ 1.4. Major Publications

Third Wave Publications (after 2010)

MARK R. LEVIN, THE LIBERTY AMENDMENTS: RESTORING THE AMERICAN REPUBLIC (2013)

Robert G. Natelson, *Counting to Two Thirds: How Close Are We to a Convention for Proposing Amendments to the Constitution?* 19 FED. SOC. REV. 51 (2018)

_____, WHY A CONVENTION FOR PROPOSING AMENDMENTS IS A "CONVENTION OF THE STATES" (Heartland Institute, 2017), *available at*
http://articlevinfocenter.com/wp-content/uploads/2018/10/Natelson-CoS-final.pdf

———, *Founding-Era Conventions and the Meaning of the Constitution's "Convention for Proposing Amendments,"* 65 FLA. L. REV. 615 (2013)

———, *James Madison and the Constitution's "Convention for Proposing Amendments,"* in UNION AND STATES' RIGHTS: A HISTORY AND INTERPRETATION OF INTERPOSITION, NULLIFICATION, AND SECESSION 150 YEARS AFTER SUMTER (Neil H. Cogan ed., 2013)

———, THE ALEC ARTICLE V HANDBOOK (Am. Legislative Exch. Council, 3d ed. 2016), *available at* http://articlevinfocenter.com/wp-content/uploads/2018/10/2016-Article-V_FINAL_WEB.pdf

———, *Proposing Constitutional Amendments by Convention: Rules Governing the Process*, 78 TENN. L. REV. 693 (2011)

———, AMENDING THE CONSTITUTION BY CONVENTION: PRACTICAL GUIDANCE FOR CITIZENS AND POLICYMAKERS (Independence Inst., 2012) (updated and amended version of an earlier paper published by the Goldwater Institute)

———, AMENDING THE CONSTITUTION BY CONVENTION: LESSONS FOR TODAY FROM THE CONSTITUTION'S FIRST CENTURY (Independence Inst., 2011) (updated and amended version of an earlier paper published by the Goldwater Institute)

———, AMENDING THE CONSTITUTION BY CONVENTION: A MORE COMPLETE VIEW OF THE FOUNDERS' PLAN (Independence Inst., 2010) (updated and amended version of an earlier paper published by the Goldwater Institute)

Michael B. Rappaport, *The Constitutionality of a Limited Convention: An Originalist Analysis*, 28 CONST. COMMENT. 53 (2012)

Michael Stern, *Reopening the Constitutional Road to Reform: Toward a Safeguarded Article V Convention*, 78 TENN. L. REV. 765 (2011)

———, *A Brief Reply to Professor Penrose*, 78 TENN. L. REV. 807 (2011)

JOHN R. VILE, CONVENTIONAL WISDOM: THE ALTERNATE ARTICLE V MECHANISM FOR PROPOSING AMENDMENTS TO THE U.S. CONSTITUTION (2016) (This work has elements of both Second and Third Wave writing.)

Second Wave Publications (superseded, but still sometimes useful)

RUSSELL L. CAPLAN, CONSTITUTIONAL BRINKMANSHIP: AMENDING THE CONSTITUTION BY NATIONAL CONVENTION (1988) (the leading Second Wave publication and an important starting point for Third Wave scholarship)

Walter Dellinger, *The Legitimacy of Constitutional Change: Rethinking the Amendment Process,* 97 HARV. L. REV. 386 (1983–1984) (correcting the view that the courts have no role in Article V)

Ann Stuart Diamond, *A Convention for Proposing Amendments: The Constitution's Other Method,* 11 STATE OF AM. FEDERALISM 113 (1980)

John M. Harmon, *Constitutional Convention: Limitation of Power to Propose Amendments to the Constitution,* 3 OP. O.L.C. 390 (1979) (an unusually thorough piece of work for its time, and the transition to Second Wave writings)

Paul Monaghan, *We the People[s], Original Understanding, and Constitutional Amendment,* 96 COLUM. L. REV. 121 (1996)

Michael Stokes Paulsen, *A General Theory of Article V: The Constitutional Lessons of the Twenty-Seventh Amendment,* 103 YALE L.J. 677 (1993)

Grover Joseph Rees III, *The Amendment Process and Limited Constitutional Conventions,* 2 BENCHMARK 66 (1986)

Ronald D. Rotunda & Stephen J. Safranek, *An Essay on Term Limits and a Call for a Constitutional Convention,* 80 MARQ. L. REV. 227 (1996–1997)

U.S. DEPT. OF JUSTICE, OFFICE OF LEGAL POLICY, LIMITED CONSTITUTIONAL CONVENTIONS UNDER ARTICLE V OF THE UNITED STATES CONSTITUTION (1987)

Bruce M. Van Sickle & Lynn M. Boughey, *A Lawful and Peaceful Revolution, Article V and Congress' Present Duty to Call a Convention for Proposing Amendments*, 14 HAMLINE L. REV. 1 (1990–1991)

First Wave Publications (no longer useful)

AMERICAN BAR ASSOCIATION, AMENDMENT OF THE CONSTITUTION BY THE CONVENTION METHOD UNDER ARTICLE V (1973) (the best researched of the First Wave publications)

Charles L. Black, Jr., *The Proposed Amendment of Article V: A Threatened Disaster*, 72 YALE L.J. 957 (1963)

———, *Amending the Constitution: A Letter to a Congressman*, 82 YALE L.J. 189 (1972)

Arthur E. Bonfield, *Proposing Constitutional Amendments by Convention: Some Problems*, 39 NOTRE DAME L. REV. 659 (1964)

———, *The Dirksen Amendment and the Article V Convention Process*, 66 MICH. L. REV. 949 (1967–1968)

Dwight W. Connely, *Amending the Constitution: Is This Any Way to Call a Constitutional Convention?*, 22 ARIZ. L. REV. 1011 (1980)

Walter E. Dellinger, *The Recurring Question of the "Limited" Constitutional Convention*, 88 YALE L.J. 1623 (1978–1979)

Sam J. Ervin, Jr., *Proposed Legislation to Implement the Convention Method of Amending the Constitution*, 66 MICH. L. REV. 875 (1967)

Bill Gaugush, *Principles Governing the Interpretation and Exercise of Article V Powers*, 35 WESTERN POL. Q. 212 (1982)

Gerald Gunther, *The Convention Method of Amending the United States Constitution*, 14 GA. L. REV. 1 (1979)

Paul G. Kauper, *The Alternative Amendment Process: Some Observations*, 66 MICH. L. REV. 903 (1967–1968)

Philip L. Martin, *The Application Clause of Article V*, 85 POL. SCI. Q. 616 (1970)

John T. Noonan, Jr., *The Convention Method of Constitutional Amendment: Its Meaning, Usefulness, and Wisdom*, 10 PAC. L.J. 641 (1979)

Note, *Proposing Amendments to the United States Constitution by Convention*, 70 HARV. L. REV. 1067 (1957)

Note, *Proposed Legislation on the Convention Method of Amending the United States*, 85 HARV. L. REV. 1612 (1972)

William F. Swindler, *The Current Challenge to Federalism: The Confederating Proposals*, 52 GEO. L.J. 1 (1963–1964)

Laurence H. Tribe, *Issues Raised by Requesting Congress to Call a Constitutional Convention to Propose a Balanced Budget Amendment*, 10 PAC. L.J. 627 (1979) (a list of questions about conventions, but without research to resolve them)

William W. Van Alstyne, *Does Article V Restrict the States to Calling Unlimited Conventions Only?—A Letter to a Colleague*, 1978 DUKE L.J. 1295 (an unusual First Wave article in that it concludes that conventions may be limited).

Part II.
Table of Cases

AFL-CIO v. Eu, 686 P.2d 609 (Cal. 1984)

Arizona State Legislature v. Arizona Independent Redistricting Commission, 135 S. Ct. 2652 (2015)

Barker v. Hazeltine, 3 F. Supp. 2d 1088 (D.S.D. 1998)

Barlotti v. Lyons, 189 P. 282 (Cal. 1920)

Bramberg v. Jones, 978 P.2d 1240 (Cal. 1999)

Burroughs v. United States, 290 U.S. 534 (1934)

Calzone v. Richard, (Mo. Cir. Ct. 2018), *available at* https://i2i.org/wp-content/uploads/2018-Calzone-v.-Richard-MO-CirCt.pdf

Coleman v. Miller, 307 U.S. 438 (1939)

Davis v. Hildebrant, 241 U.S. 565 (1916)

Decher v. Secretary of State, 177 N.W. 288 (Mich. 1920)

Dillon v. Gloss, 256 U.S. 368 (1921).

Dodge v. Woolsey, 59 U.S. 331 (1855)

Donovan v. Priest, 931 S.W.2d 119 (Ark. 1996)

Dyer v. Blair, 390 F. Supp. 1291 (N.D. Ill. 1975)

Field v. Clark, 143 U.S. 649 (1892)

Fitzgerald v.Greene, 134 U.S. 377 (1890)

Goldwater v. Carter, 444 U.S. 996 (1979)

Gralike v. Cooke, 191 F.3d 911 (8th Cir. 1999), *aff'd on other grounds*, 531 U.S. 510 (2001)

Hawke v. Smith ("Hawke I"), 253 U.S. 221 (1920)

Hawke v. Smith ("Hawke II"), 253 U.S. 231 (1920)

Herbring v. Brown, 180 P. 328 (Or. 1919)

Hollingsworth v. Virginia, 3 U.S. (3 Dall.) 378 (1798)

Idaho v. Freeman, 529 F. Supp. 1107 (D. Idaho 1981), *judgment vacated as moot sub nom.* Carmen v. Idaho, 459 U.S. 809 (1982)
In re Initiative Petition 364, 930 P.2d 186 (Okla. 1996)
Kimble v. Swackhamer, 439 U.S. 1385 (1978)
League of Women Voters v. Gwadosky, 966 F. Supp. 52 (D. Me. 1997)
Leser v. Garnett, 258 U.S. 130 (1922)
Miller v. Moore, 169 F.3d 1119 (8th Cir. 1999)
Morrissey v. State, 951 P.2d 911 (Colo. 1998)
National Federation of Independent Business v. Sebelius, 567 U.S. 599 (2012)
Oldknow v. Wainright, [K.B. 1760] 2 Burr. 1017, 97 Eng. Rep. 683
Opinion of the Justices to the Senate, 366 N.E.2d 1226 (Mass. 1977)
Opinion of the Justices, 172 S.E. 474 (N.C. 1933)
Opinion of the Justices, 673 A.2d 693 (Me. 1996)
Opinion of the Justices, 167 A. 176 (Me. 1933)
Opinion of the Justices, 107 A. 673 (Me. 1919)
Opinion of the Justices, 148 So. 107 (Ala. 1933)
Powell v. McCormick, 395 U.S. 486 (1969)
Prior v. Norland, 188 P. 727 (Colo. 1920)
Ray v. Blair, 343 U.S. 214 (1952)
Rhode Island v. Palmer ("National Prohibition Cases"), 253 U.S. 350 (1920)
Simpson v. Cenarrusa, 944 P.2d 1372 (Idaho 1997)
Smiley v. Holm, 285 U.S. 355 (1932)
Smith v. Union Bank, 30 U.S. 518 (1831)
Spriggs v. Clark, 14 P.2d 667 (Wyo. 1932)
State *ex rel.* Tate v. Sevier, 62 S.W.2d 895 (Mo. 1933)
State *ex rel.* Donnelly v. Myers, 186 N.E. 918 (Ohio 1933)
State *ex rel.* Erkenbrecher v. Cox, 257 F. 334 (D.C. Ohio 1919)
State *ex rel.* Harper v. Waltermire, 691 P.2d 826 (Mont. 1984)
State v. Hatch, 526 P.2d 1369 (Mont. 1974)
Trombetta v. Florida, 353 F. Supp. 575 (M.D. Fla. 1973)
U.S. Term Limits v. Thornton, 514 U.S. 779 (1995)
United States v. Chambers, 291 U.S. 217 (1934)
United States v. Gugel, 119 F. Supp. 897 (E.D. Ky. 1954)

United States v. Sprague, 282 U.S. 716 (1931)
United States v. Thibault, 47 F.2d 169 (2d Cir. 1931)
United States *ex rel.* Widenmann v. Colby, 265 F. 998 (D.C. Cir. 1920), *aff'd*, 253 U.S. 350 (1921)
White v. Hart, 80 U.S. 646 (1871)

Part III.
Explanatory Text with Footnotes

§ 3.1. Historical Background[20]

In seventeenth and eighteenth century Anglo-American practice, a "convention" was an assembly, other than a legislature, convened *ad hoc* to address one or more political problems.[21] In England, conventions re-enthroned the Stuart royal line in 1660[22] and granted the throne to William and Mary in 1689.[23] The latter convention promulgated the English Declaration of Rights.

Americans also began to meet in conventions during the late seventeenth century. Many conventions were bodies that convened only within a particular colony or state. However, all those that involved more than one colony or state took the forms of diplomatic

---

[20] On this history, see generally Natelson, *Conventions, supra* note 2.

[21] Natelson, *Conventions, supra* note 2 at 624; Robert G. Natelson, *Proposing Constitutional Amendments by Convention: Rules Governing the Process*, 78 TENN. L. REV. 693, 706 (2011) [hereinafter Natelson, *Rules*]; *cf.* Opinion of the Justices, 167 A. 176, 179 (Me. 1933) ("The principal distinction between a convention and a Legislature is that the former is called for a specific purpose, the latter for general purposes.")

[22] *See* 8 HOUSE OF COMMONS JOURNAL 16–18 (1660), *available at* http://www.british-history.ac.uk/search/series/commons-jrnl; *id.* at 341, *available at* https://www.british-history.ac.uk/commons-jrnl/vol8/pp341-342 (referring to those proceedings as occurring during a "convention".

[23] *See* RUSSELL L. CAPLAN, CONSTITUTIONAL BRINKMANSHIP: AMENDING THE CONSTITUTION BY NATIONAL CONVENTION 6–40 (1988) [hereinafter CONSTITUTIONAL BRINKMANSHIP].

assemblies of delegations from colonial or state governments. Sometimes other sovereignties, such as the British Crown or Iroquois tribes, participated. In imitation of international law practice, such an assembly often was called a "congress." In this context, the term "congress" meant an intergovernmental convention.

We have records of about twenty inter-colonial conventions before Independence and of eleven conventions of states from 1776 through 1787.[24] The eleven conventions of states met in Providence, Rhode Island at the end of 1776 and the beginning of 1777 and again in 1781; in Springfield, Massachusetts and York Town, Pennsylvania in 1777; in New Haven, Connecticut in 1778; in Hartford, Connecticut in 1779 and again in 1780; in Boston in 1780; in Philadelphia in 1780 and 1787; and in Annapolis in 1786.

These multi-government or "federal" conventions developed standard protocols.[25] The procedure would begin when a colony or state (or, less commonly, the Continental Congress or a prior convention) issued an invitation to other governments to meet at a prescribed place and time to discuss one or more subjects. The subjects might include Indian affairs, common defense, war supply, inflation, trade, or other topics.

During the eighteenth century, an "application" was merely an address to another person or entity. The word sometimes referred to an invitation to a convention and sometimes to a request to another entity to issue an invitation. The invitation itself was a special kind of application,[26] and usually was denominated a *call*.[27]

---

[24] Robert G. Natelson, *List of Conventions of States and Colonies in American History*, http://articlevinfocenter.com/list-conventions-states-colonies-american-history/.

[25] These are discussed generally in Natelson, *Conventions, supra* note 2.

[26] *Id.*, at 667.

[27] On terminology, see *id.*, at 629–32. For an example of the term "application" being used as a synonym for "call," see *id.* at 642 (reproducing a letter from the then-president of Massachusetts leading to the 1776–1777 Providence Convention). For additional terminology, see Natelson, *Rules, supra* note 21, at 698–99, 708.

A proposed convention might be *partial*—meaning limited to the governments in a certain region of the country—or *general*, meaning inclusive of all or most colonies or states. The procedures for partial and general conventions were identical.

Because these were meetings among governments, the protocols were based on those prevailing in international law for meetings among sovereigns.[28] Each colony or state sent a *committee* (delegation) of *commissioners* (delegates) empowered by documents called *commissions* or *credentials* and often by *instructions* (usually secret) as well. The call, commissions, and instructions defined the outer scope of the commissioners' powers. At the conclave, each government received one vote, irrespective of the size of its committee. The convention elected its own officers and established its own rules.

Many of the Constitution's framers and leading ratifiers had served as commissioners to multi-government conventions. Others were familiar with the process from their experience in government service. Article V's "Convention for proposing Amendments" was modeled after these conclaves and was designed to be a convention of the states.[29] Indeed, the phrase "convention of the states" and similar expressions[30] remained the usual way of referring to an Article V amendments convention for many decades after the Constitution was ratified.

During the two centuries following ratification, states continued to meet in conventions. The 1814 Hartford Convention was a "partial" (regional) gathering of delegates from the New England states designed to coordinate the response among those states to the unpop-

---

[28] CONSTITUTIONAL BRINKSMANSHIP, *supra* note 23, at 95–96 (1988).

[29] Natelson, *Conventions, supra* note 2, at 680–85.

[30] Smith v. Union Bank, 30 U.S. 518, 528 (1831) (referring to an amendments convention as a "convention of the states"). *See also* Natelson, *Conventions, supra* note 2, at 684–85 (reproducing language of early state applications and a responsive resolution) and ROBERT G. NATELSON, WHY A CONVENTION FOR PROPOSING AMENDMENTS IS A "CONVENTION OF THE STATES" (Heartland Institute, 2017), *available at* http://articlevinfocenter.com/wp-content/uploads/2018/10/Natelson-CoS-final.pdf.

ular War of 1812. It endorsed a series of amendments to the Constitution.[31] Because, however, it met outside the sanction of Article V, it could not issue ratifiable proposals. Another regional convention was the gathering of nine states at Nashville, Tennessee in 1850. It sought to coordinate Southern response to federal policy.[32] The seven-state Montgomery, Alabama convention of 1861 met to organize Southern secession and draft a new Confederate constitution. In 1889, nine states convened in St. Louis, Missouri to develop a common approach to anti-competitive practices in the meat-packing industry.[33] Finally, several conventions of Western states (formally called "commissions") met during the twentieth century to negotiate water compacts.[34] The most important of these was the "Colorado River Commission," which assembled, primarily in Santa Fe, New Mexico, to frame the Colorado River Compact.

Since the Founding, there have been two "general" conventions. The 1861 Washington Conference Convention was the largest convention of states ever held. Its purpose was to propose a constitutional amendment to stave off the Civil War.[35] Because it met

---

[31] *Amendments to the Constitution Proposed by the Hartford Convention: 1814*, YALE LAW SCHOOL, http://avalon.law.yale.edu/19th_century/hartconv.asp (last visited Oct. 10, 2018). The journal is also available in A SHORT ACCOUNT OF THE HARTFORD CONVENTION (Theodore Lyman ed., 1823).

[32] *See* THELMA JENNINGS, THE NASHVILLE CONVENTION: SOUTHERN MOVEMENT FOR UNITY, 1848–1850 (1980). This gathering, called by the State of Mississippi, also was known as the Southern Convention.

[33] *Newly Rediscovered; The 1889 St. Louis Convention of States*, http://articlevinfocenter.com/newly-rediscovered-1889-st-louis-convention-states/.

[34] Robert G. Natelson, *List of Conventions of States and Colonies in American History*, http://articlevinfocenter.com/list-conventions-states-colonies-american-history/.

[35] The official name of the gathering was the Washington Conference Convention, but it is also commonly referred to as the "Washington Peace Conference." It was called by Virginia, and attended by twenty-one states after several already had seceded. Former President John Tyler served as convention president.

outside Article V, it could not issue its proposal to the states directly, so it sought action from Congress, which was not forthcoming. In 2017, a general convention with nineteen states in attendance met in Phoenix, Arizona to draft recommended rules for a future Article V conclave. The Phoenix Planning Convention[36] was the first genuine convention of states to include female commissioners—and the first to be chaired by a woman: Arizona State Representative Kelly Townsend.

All these gatherings generally followed the convention protocols established during the seventeenth and eighteenth centuries.[37] The 1861 Washington, D.C. assembly mimicked an Article V convention for proposing amendments in almost every particular.

§ 3.2. Types of Conventions

For constitutional purposes, one can classify conventions sponsored by American governments in several different ways: in-state and multi-state; conventions to propose, to ratify, and to do both; and conventions whose powers are plenipotentiary or limited.

The proceedings are collected in A REPORT OF THE DEBATES AND PROCEEDINGS IN THE SECRET SESSIONS IN THE CONFERENCE CONVENTION FOR PROPOSING AMENDMENTS TO THE CONSTITUTION OF THE UNITED STATES (L.E. Chittenden ed., 1861) [hereinafter WASHINGTON CONFERENCE REPORT]. For a modern treatment, see ROBERT GRAY GUNDERSON, OLD GENTLEMEN'S CONVENTION: THE WASHINGTON PEACE CONFERENCE OF 1861 (1961). (The name of the book comes from a derogatory comment by abolitionist Horace Greeley.)

[36] The formal name for the assembly was the Balanced Budget Amendment Planning Convention. JOURNAL, *supra* note 11(unpaginated, but providing full title on sheet 7).

[37] The journal of the 1814 Hartford Convention does not reveal how votes were tabulated (by commissioner or by state), but otherwise its proceedings are consistent.

§ 3.2.1. In-State and Multi-State Conventions

An *in-state convention* is a meeting of delegates from a single state. One example is a state constitutional convention; another is a state convention of the kind that ratified the Twenty-First Amendment. In such gatherings, delegates usually are popularly elected by, and represent, the people—although during the Founding Era there were some in-state conventions composed of delegations from towns or other local governments. The Constitution authorizes two kinds of in-state conventions: those authorized to ratify the Constitution and those authorized to ratify amendments.[38]

By contrast, a *multi-state*, *interstate*, or *federal* convention is a gathering of representatives from states or from state legislatures.

§ 3.2.2. Proposing and Ratifying Conventions

A *proposing convention* is charged only with proposing solutions to prescribed problems. As its name suggests, the convention for proposing amendments a proposing convention. Other proposing conventions include the 1787 Constitutional Convention, the 1861 Washington Conference Convention, and the 2017 Phoenix Planning Convention.

A *ratifying convention* is charged only with ratifying or rejecting specific proposals. Examples of ratifying conventions are the in-state assemblies that approved the Constitution[39] and those that approved the Twenty-First Amendment (repealing Prohibition).[40]

During the Revolutionary War, some in-state conventions enjoyed both proposing and ratifying power, particularly in states

---

[38] U.S. CONST. arts. V, VII.

[39] U.S. CONST., art. VII.

[40] On the latter, see RATIFICATION OF THE TWENTY-FIRST AMENDMENT TO THE CONSTITUTION OF THE UNITED STATES: STATE CONVENTION RECORDS AND LAWS (Everett Somerville Brown ed., 1938). For a shorter treatment, see Everett Somerville Brown, *The Ratification of the Twenty-First Amendment*, 29 AM. POL. SCI. REV. 1005 (1935).

whose legislatures were not functioning.[41] By contrast, most multi-state conventions were authorized to propose only. However, the 1780 Philadelphia Price Convention was empowered to both propose and decide,[42] and an early draft of the Constitution would have granted an amendments convention authority to both propose and decide. The Framers ultimately rejected that approach.[43]

§ 3.2.3. Plenipotentiary and Limited Conventions

A *plenipotentiary* convention is one with an unlimited mandate, or at least a mandate that is very broad. The term comes from international diplomatic practice. During the Founding Era, the in-state conventions that managed their governments in absence of the legislature enjoyed plenipotentiary authority. The Constitution does not authorize any plenipotentiary conventions.

A *limited* convention is restricted to one or more topics. The limited convention with the narrowest agenda is a ratifying convention, whose only power is to approve or reject a preset proposal.

Historically, multi-state proposing conventions have been authorized to deliberate, debate, draft, and recommend (or, in a few cases, to mandate) solutions to prescribed problems. Sometimes the prescribed agenda has been very broad, as in the case of the First Continental Congress (1774). On other occasions the agenda has been very narrow. For example, the 1781 Providence Convention was confined to New England military supply issues for a single year. But in no case has a proposal convention been limited to approving or disapproving prescribed language. That would inhibit the deliberative

---

[41] The division between proposal and decision was elucidated by the seventeenth century political author James Harrington in his *Commonwealth of Oceana*—a work hugely popular among the Founders. Harrington compared it to the common domestic situation in which one girl cuts a cake while the other gets to choose which piece is hers. He therefore referred to it as "dividing" and "choosing."

[42] Robert G. Natelson, *Conventions, supra* note 2.

[43] *Id.* at 621–22.

purpose of a proposal convention, and would ill-suit the dignity of an assembly of semi-sovereigns.

§ 3.2.4. Categorizing the Constitutional Convention and the Convention for Proposing Amendments

The Constitutional Convention

There is an oft-repeated claim that Congress called the 1787 Constitutional Convention and restricted it to amending the Articles. That claim is erroneous.[44]

What actually happened was that the 1786 Annapolis Convention issued a resolution somewhat analogous to an Article V application, but addressed to its participating states rather than to Congress. The resolution asked the states to call and attend another, wider convention.[45] Accordingly, Virginia called a federal convention for May of 1787.[46] Neither the Annapolis resolution nor the state calls nor the convention itself proceeded under the Articles of Confederation. Rather, they were exercises of the states' reserved powers.[47] Nor was the convention restricted to proposing

---

[44] After most of the states already had accepted Virginia's invitation to participate, Congress passed a weak resolution expressing the "opinion" that the convention be limited to amending the Articles. All but two states disregarded this "opinion," but many writers have confused it with the convention call. *Id.*, at 674–79. For a complete review of the historical record, see Michael Farris, *Defying Conventional Wisdom: The Constitution Was Not the Product of a Runaway Convention*, 40 HARVARD J. L. & PUB. POL'Y 61 (2017).

[45] *Proceedings of Commissioners to Remedy Defects of the Federal Government* (1786), http://avalon.law.yale.edu/18th_century/annapoli.asp.

[46] Article V Information Center, *Who Called the Constitutional Convention? Answer: The Commonwealth of Virginia*, http://articlevinfocenter.com/who-called-the-constitutional-convention-answer-the-commonwealth-of-virginia/.

[47] The Articles did not empower the Confederation Congress to call such a convention, so the Articles reserved that power to the states. ARTS. OF CONFED., art. II ("Each state retains . . . every power, jurisdiction, and right,

amendments to the Articles. Both the call and the commissions issued by ten of the twelve participating states empowered the convention to recommend any and all expedient changes to the "foederal constitution."[48] (At the time, the word "constitution" referred to the entire political system.[49])

The 1787 gathering in Philadelphia was obviously a *multi-state* or *federal* convention rather than one limited to a single state. Just as obviously, it was a proposing rather than a ratifying body. Although technically limited, the breadth of its charge caused it to lean toward the *plenipotentiary* side.

The Convention for Proposing Amendments

This also is a *multi-state* gathering. Although some writers have depicted it as a popularly-elected assembly similar to an in-state convention, it is actually a *convention of the states*: On this point, the evidence is overwhelming and uncontradicted,[50] and confirmed by a Supreme Court pronouncement.[51]

---

which is not by this Confederation expressly delegated to the United States, in Congress assembled.").

[48] 3 THE RECORDS OF THE FEDERAL CONVENTION OF 1787, at 559–86 (Max Farrand ed., 1937) (hereinafter called FARRAND'S RECORDS).

[49] *See, e.g.*, THOMAS SHERIDAN, A COMPLETE DICTIONARY OF THE ENGLISH LANGUAGE (1789) (unpaginated) (defining the legal meanings of "constitution" as "established form of government, system of laws and customs; particular law, establishment, institution"); *cf.* DECLARATION OF INDEPENDENCE ("foreign to our Constitution"); HENRY ST. JOHN, VISCOUNT BOLINGBROKE, ON PARTIES 141 (11th ed, 1786) ("By constitution we mean, whenever we speak with propriety and exactness, the assemblage of laws, institutions and customs . . . that compose the general system, according to which the community hath agreed to be governed."). Bolingbroke was one of the most influential political commentators and philosophers of the eighteenth century.

[50] ROBERT G. NATELSON, WHY A CONVENTION FOR PROPOSING AMENDMENTS IS A "CONVENTION OF THE STATES" (Heartland Institute, 2017), *available at* http://articlevinfocenter.com/wp-content/uploads/2018/10/Natelson-CoS-final.pdf (collecting historical and structural evidence, including state legis-

Unlike the Constitutional Convention, which states called in their sovereign capacities, a convention for proposing amendments is called pursuant to the Constitution. It draws its authority from the Constitution and only to the extent permitted by the applications and calls. Its authority is therefore limited to the scope of those documents, and is consequently narrower than the authority of a constitutional convention. On the other hand, the fact that it is a *proposing* body suggests that its discretion cannot be confined to approving or rejecting prescribed language, as in the case of a ratifying convention.

§ 3.3. Why the Founders Adopted the Proposal Convention in Article V.

An early draft of the Constitution permitted amendments to be proposed and adopted only by a multi-state convention.[52] Then the Framers added provisions allowing Congress to propose amendments and requiring state ratification.[53] Congress received the power to propose because the Framers believed that Congress's position would enable it readily to see defects in the system.

However, some delegates—notably George Mason of Virginia—pointed out that Congress might become abusive or exceed its powers.[54] It might refuse to adopt a necessary or desirable amendment,

---

lative materials from the ratification era characterizing a convention for proposing amendments as a convention of the states). The first legislative application similarly characterizes the convention. 1 ANNALS OF CONGRESS 28–29 (1789) (Joseph Gales ed., 1834) (reproducing Virginia application of Nov. 14, 1788, calling an amendments convention "a convention of the states").

[51] *Smith v. Union Bank*, 30 U.S. 518, 528 (1831); see also Calzone v. Richard, (Mo. Cir. Ct. 2018), *available at* https://i2i.org/wp-content/uploads/2018-Calzone-v.-Richard-MO-CirCt.pdf (referring to a convention for proposing amendments as "a convention of the states").

[52] 2 FARRAND'S RECORDS, *supra* note 48, at 159.

[53] *Id.* at 578.

[54] *Id.* at 649.

particularly one designed to curb its own authority. Accordingly, the Framers inserted the convention for proposing amendments as a way for the states to present corrective amendments for ratification without substantive congressional participation.[55]

The function of the application and convention process as a "congressional bypass" was discussed at length during the debates over the ratification of the Constitution. James Madison addressed the issue succinctly in *The Federalist No. 43*: The Constitution, he wrote, "equally enables the General, and the State Governments, to originate the amendment of errors, as they may be pointed out by the experience on one side or on the other."[56]

Although that statement has been much quoted, comments by other Founders are more helpful for understanding the full purpose and scope of the application and convention procedure. Samuel Rose was a New York state legislator and initially a moderate antifederalist, but he ultimately supported the Constitution at his state's ratifying convention. He explained the purpose behind the alternative proposal procedures in this way:

> The reason why there are two modes of obtaining amendments prescribed by the constitution I suppose to be this—it could not be known to the framers of the constitution, whether there was too much power given by it or too little; they therefore prescribed a mode by which Congress might procure more, if in the operation of the government it was found necessary; and they prescribed for the states a mode of restraining the powers of

---

[55] On the framing process, see Robert G. Natelson, *Conventions, supra* note 2, at 621–24; Natelson, *Rules, supra* note 21, at 699–702; Michael Stern, *Reopening the Constitutional Road to Reform: Toward a Safeguarded Article V Convention*, 78 TENN. L. REV. 765, 767–70 (2011) [hereinafter *Stern, Reopening*]; see also Idaho v. Freeman, 529 F. Supp. 1107, 1132 (D. Idaho 1981), *judgment vacated as moot sub nom.* Carmen v. Idaho, 459 U.S. 809 (1982) ("[T]he drafters of the Constitution found it appropriate to grant the same power to propose amendments to both the local [state] and national governments. . . .").

[56] Despite the reference to "states," the applying entities are actually the state legislatures acting alone, not the state governments. *See infra* § 3.7.

government, if upon trial it should be found that they had given too much.[57]

A still more complete treatment was provided by Tench Coxe, a Philadelphia businessman who served in the Confederation Congress and, after the Constitution's ratification, as Alexander Hamilton's assistant secretary of the treasury. During the ratification debates, Coxe was one of the most influential pro-Constitution essayists. He explained the amendment process in this way:

> Before we dismiss this point, it will be necessary to attend very particularly to one more fact relating to it. The sovereign power of altering and amending the constitution, or supreme law of the American confederacy, does not lie with this foederal legislature, whom some have erroneously apprehended to be supreme. That power, which is truly and evidently the real point of sovereignty, is vested in the several legislatures and [ratifying] conventions of the states, chosen by the people respectively within them. The foederal government cannot alter the constitution, the people at large by their own agency cannot alter the constitution, but the representative bodies of the states, that is their legislatures and conventions, only can execute these acts of sovereign power.
>
> From the foregoing circumstances results another reflection equally satisfactory and important, which is, that as the foederal legislature cannot effect dangerous alterations which they might desire, so they cannot prevent such wholesome alterations and amendments as are now desired, or which experience may hereafter suggest. Let us suppose any one or more alterations to be in contemplation by the people at large, or by the state legislatures. If two thirds of those legislatures require it, Congress must call a general convention, even though they dislike the proposed amendments, and if three fourths of the state legislatures or conventions approve such proposed amendments, they become an actual and binding part of the constitution, without any possible interference of Congress.

---

[57] 23 THE DOCUMENTARY HISTORY OF THE RATIFICATION OF THE CONSTITUTION 2520–22 (Merrill Jensen, John P. Kaminsky, & Gaspare J. Saladino eds., 2009).

If then, contrary to the opinion of the eight adopting states, the foederal government should prove dangerous, it seems the members of the confederacy will have a full and uncontroulable power to alter its nature, and render it completely safe and useful.[58]

§ 3.4. Analyzing the Text of Article V

Article V of the Constitution can be divided into four distinct parts, designated below by different type faces:

<u>The Congress, whenever two thirds of both Houses shall deem it necessary, shall propose Amendments to this Constitution, or, on the Application of the Legislatures of two thirds of the several States, shall call a Convention for proposing Amendments,</u> *which, in either Case, shall be valid to all Intents and Purposes, as Part of this Constitution, when ratified by the Legislatures of three fourths of the several States, or by Convention in three fourths thereof,* **as the one or the other Mode of Ratification may be proposed by the Congress;** Provided that no Amendment which may be made prior to the Year One thousand eight hundred and eight shall in any Manner affect the first and fourth Clauses in the

---

[58] Tench Coxe, *A Pennsylvanian to the Convention of the State of New York*, Jun. 11, 1788, *reprinted in* 20 *id.*, at 1139, 1142–43; see also Tench Coxe, *A Friend of Society and Liberty*, PA. GAZETTE, July 23, 1788, *reprinted in* 18 *id.* at 277, 284:

> It must therefore be evident to every candid man, that two thirds of the states can *always* procure a general convention for the purpose of amending the constitution, and that three fourths of them can introduce those amendments into the constitution, although the President, Senate and Foederal House of Representatives, should be *unanimously* opposed to each and all of them. Congress therefore cannot hold any *power*, which three fourths of the states shall not approve, on *experience.*

(Italics in original.)

Ninth Section of the first Article; and that no State, without its Consent, shall be deprived of its equal Suffrage in the Senate.

The underlined language is the procedure by which amendments are formally proposed. Formal proposal is a condition precedent to the remaining steps, so it occurs first in the amendment process.

The **bolded** language, although placed third, occurs second in the amendment process, when Congress designates a "Mode of Ratification" for formal proposals. Obviously, Congress has no authority to designate a mode of ratification unless the potential amendment has been properly proposed.

The *italicized* language outlines the ratification process, which occurs only after proposal and congressional selection of the mode of ratification.

The final proviso, set forth in ordinary roman type, prohibits certain kinds of amendments. It is a reminder that the Article V procedure is carried out subject to what Madison called "the forms of the Constitution."[59] One cannot use Article V to obtain unconstitutional results. For example, neither Congress nor a convention for proposing amendments has power to alter the ratification procedure, as alarmists sometimes suggest. Any effort by the convention to do would be ignored by other agencies of government, including the courts.

Now, let us focus on the proposal and ratification portions of Article V:

> The Congress, whenever two thirds of both Houses shall deem it necessary, shall propose Amendments to this Constitution, or, on the Application of the Legislatures of two thirds of the several States, shall call a Convention for proposing Amendments, *which, in either Case, shall be valid to all Intents and Purposes, as Part of this Constitution, when ratified by the Legislatures of three*

---

[59] Letter from James Madison to George Turberville (Nov. 2, 1788), *reprinted in* 5 THE WRITINGS OF JAMES MADISON 297, 299 (Gaillard Hunt ed., 1904); *Cf.* Michael B. Rappaport, *The Constitutionality of a Limited Convention: An Originalist Analysis*, 28 CONST. COMMENT. 53, 92–93 (2012).

fourths of the several States, or by Convention in three fourths thereof....

Observe that Article V provides two methods of proposal and two methods of ratification. Both methods of ratification have been employed: State conventions ratified the Twenty-First Amendment and state legislatures ratified all the rest. The congressional method of proposal has been used to completion, but the state application and convention method has not. Let us focus on the language that governs the latter: "[O]n the Application of the Legislatures of two thirds of the several States, [Congress] shall call a Convention for proposing Amendments...."

The following is clear from the language:

- If two thirds of the states make "Application" to Congress for a convention,
- Congress "shall" (must) "call" one, and
- The power granted to the convention is "proposing Amendments."

Although the text of Article V contains much explicit guidance, commentators, particularly those who oppose holding any amendments convention, have long complained that the language of Article V is insufficiently detailed.[60] What they overlook is that the language of Article V is no less detailed than most provisions in the Constitution. The Framers sought to keep the document short by outlining the basics and leaving to readers the task of supplementing the text by consulting contemporaneous law and historical practice. For example, Article I, Section 9, Clause 2 of the Constitution states that "The privilege of the writ of habeas corpus shall not be suspended . . ." That Clause does not explain what a writ of habeas corpus is, what it

---

[60] *E.g.*, Laurence H. Tribe, *Issues Raised by Requesting Congress to Call a Constitutional Convention to Propose a Balanced Budget Amendment*, 10 PAC. L.J. 627, 632 (1979) (calling the Constitution's convention wording "strikingly vague").

contains, how it is issued, or the traditional rules regarding suspension. The same might be said of the constitutional guarantees of trial by jury. Readers are expected to do sufficient homework to ascertain those details for themselves. Complaints about the lack of detail in Article V invariably come from those who have not bothered to do their homework.

In interpreting Article V, the judiciary has, quite properly, relied heavily on historical practice. In answering questions not answered directly by the text, we shall do the same.

§ 3.5. Applicable Legal Principles: Interpretation, Incidental Powers, and Fiduciary Obligations

Contrary to some suggestions,[61] Article V questions are freely justiciable.[62] Indeed, "the judiciary . . . has . . . dealt with virtually all the significant portions of that article,"[63] and the courts apply similar rules of interpretation to Article V as to other parts of the Constitution. If there is a difference between judicial interpretation of Article V and that of other parts of the Constitution, it is that interpretation of

---

[61] Some writers cite stray Supreme Court dicta or concurrences suggesting that congressional control over the amendment process is unreviewable. The language cited appears in *White v. Hart*, 80 U.S. 649 (1871), and *Coleman v. Miller*, 307 U.S. 438, 456 (1939) (Black, J., concurring).

Black's *Coleman* concurrence has had a disproportionate effect on public perceptions, considering (1) the patent implausibility of its core claim (it asserted, in the teeth of the constitutional language, that *Congress* has absolute control of the amendment process), see *Idaho v. Freeman*, 529 F. Supp. 1107, 1135–36 (D. Idaho 1981), judgment vacated as moot sub nom. *Carmen v. Idaho*, 459 U.S. 809 (1982), (2) that it was not the opinion of the Court, (3) that it has never been followed and (4) that the courts have universally repudiated it!

[62] Opinion of the Justices, 172 S.E. 474 (N.C. 1933) (stating that whether an amendment is ratified ultimately is determined by the Supreme Court); Dyer v. Blair, 390 F. Supp. 1291 (N.D. Ill. 1975) (Stevens, J.); *Freeman*, 529 F. Supp. 1107. See also the Article V cases cited throughout this book. *See supra* Part II.

[63] *Freeman*, 529 F. Supp. at 1126.

Article V is more traditional than the sometimes freewheeling approach the Supreme Court adopts when construing the Commerce Power or the Due Process Clauses.

When Article V's language is indisputably clear—such as the grant of discretion to Congress to select a mode of ratification[64]—the clear language is enforced.[65] When the meaning is less obvious, courts consult Founding-Era evidence of meaning and, on occasion, evidence of subsequent usage.[66]

The Supreme Court observed in one Article V case that "with the Constitution or other written instrument, what is reasonably implied is as much a part of it as what is expressed."[67] Just as the Constitution's other express grants carry with them incidental powers,[68]

---

[64] United States v. Sprague, 282 U.S. 716 (1931). The language in *Sprague* was arguably, broader—that all of Article V precluded interpretation—but other parts of Article V were not at issue. *See Coleman*, 307 U.S. 438 (referring to the "familiar principle, what was there said must be read in the light of the point decided"). As the footnotes in this work demonstrate, the courts, including the Supreme Court, have freely interpreted the less-obvious portions of the Article.

[65] Hawke v. Smith ("Hawke I"), 253 U.S. 221 (1920).

[66] Leser v. Garnett, 258 U.S. 130 (1922) (relying on history to affirm validity of the procedure adopted for the Fifteenth, and therefore the Nineteenth, Amendment); Hollingsworth v. Virginia, 3 U.S. (3 Dall.) 381 (1798) (following practice pertaining to first ten amendments); *Dyer*, 390 F. Supp. at 1306–07 (applying historical evidence in determining how conventions determine voting rules); United States v. Gugel, 119 F. Supp. 897 (E.D. Ky. 1954) (citing history of judicial reliance on the Fourteenth Amendment as evidence that it had been validly adopted); Barlotti v. Lyons, 189 P. 282 (Cal. 1920) (citing Founding-Era evidence in defining the Article V word "legislature"); Opinion of the Justices, 167 A. 176, 179 (Me. 1933) (determining the mode of election for a state ratifying convention by consulting historical practice).

[67] Dillon v. Gloss, 256 U.S. 368, 373 (1921) (holding that Congress has power to limit time for ratification as incidental to its selection of a mode of ratification).

[68] Natelson, *Rules, supra* note 21, at 704–06. The Founding-Era law of principals and incidents and its implication for constitutional interpretation

so do the grants in Article V.[69] In other words, a grant of power to an assembly operating under Article V carries with it subordinate powers that, at the time the Constitution was adopted, customarily accompanied such a grant, or are otherwise reasonably necessary to carrying out the grant.[70]

The Article V process includes some agency relationships. Congress serves as an agent for the states in counting applications and calling the convention. Commissioners at the convention serve as agents for their respective state legislatures. Traditional convention practice tells us that normal rules of fiduciary conduct apply in these relationships.[71] These include (1) an obligation by Congress to treat all of its principals (the state legislatures) impartially, (2) obligations by commissioners to remain within the scope of their powers and otherwise obey instructions, and (3) the power of state legislatures to recall commissioners.

---

are discussed in Robert G. Natelson, *The Legal Origins of the Necessary and Proper Clause*, in THE ORIGINS OF THE NECESSARY AND PROPER CLAUSE 52, 60–68 (2010). The basic concepts outlined there were adopted by Chief Justice Roberts in his discussion of the Clause in *National Federation of Independent Business v. Sebelius*, 567 U.S. 599-61 (2012).

[69] *Dillon*, 256 U.S. at 373 (holding that Congress has power to limit time for ratification as incidental to its selection of a mode of ratification); *State ex rel. Tate v. Sevier*, 62 S.W.2d 895 (Mo. 1933) (holding that Article V gives state legislatures power to provide for ratifying conventions); *State ex rel. Donnelly v. Myers*, 186 N.E. 918 (Ohio 1933) (stating that the calling of a convention is an incidental duty of the state legislature when Congress chooses that mode of ratification). From the holding in *Donnelly* it follows that the power to constitute ratifying conventions is not, as sometimes claimed, lodged in Congress.

[70] *Myers*, 186 N.E. 918 (stating that the calling of a convention is a duty of the state legislature when Congress chooses that mode of ratification because it is "necessary and incidental" to ratification); *see also Sevier*, 62 S.W.2d 895 (holding that Article V gives state legislatures power to provide for ratifying conventions).

[71] Natelson, *Rules, supra* note 21, at 703–04.

§ 3.6. Assemblies Acting under Article V Do So Solely by Virtue of Powers Granted by Article V.

Like some other parts of the Constitution, Article V grants a list of enumerated powers. The grants are made to designated assemblies: legislatures and conventions.[72]

The grants under Article V, together with their incidental powers, are the sole source of authority for amending the Constitution.[73] Thus, Congress holds no authority over the amending process by virtue of other grants in the Constitution.[74] Because the amending power was created by the Constitution and did not antedate it,[75] the state legislatures hold no amending power by virtue of authority reserved under the Tenth Amendment.[76] The law governing the amendment process is federal, not state, law.[77]

The principles set forth in the prior paragraph are worth emphasizing because some Article V activists have assumed

---

[72] Hawke v. Smith ("Hawke I"), 253 U.S. 221 (1920); *see also* Hawke v. Smith ("Hawke II"), 253 U.S. 231 (1920).

[73] Prior v. Norland, 188 P. 729 (Colo. 1920).

[74] Idaho v. Freeman, 529 F. Supp. 1107, 1127-28 (D. Idaho 1981), *judgment vacated as moot sub nom.* Carmen v. Idaho, 459 U.S. 809 (1982) ("In proposing or acting on a proposed constitutional amendment Congress is not acting pursuant to its 'ordinary' legislative powers found in article I but acts according to those powers granted under article V) (relying on Hollingsworth v. Virginia, 3 U.S. 376 (1798)); *id.* at 1151 ("Thus, Congress, outside of the authority granted by article V, has no power to act with regard to an amendment, i.e., it does not retain any of its traditional authority vested in it by article I").

[75] *Cf.* U.S. Term Limits v. Thornton, 514 U.S. 779 (1995).

[76] United States v. Sprague, 282 U.S. 716, 733 (1931) (holding the Tenth Amendment irrelevant because, "The fifth article does not purport to delegate any governmental power to the United States.... On the contrary... the article is a grant of authority by the people to Congress, and not to the United States."); United States v. Thibault, 47 F.2d 169 (2d Cir. 1931) (holding that Tenth Amendment is not relevant in the ratification process); Opinion of the Justices to the Senate, 366 N.E.2d 1226 (Mass. 1977); *Dyer v. Blair*, 390 F. Supp. 1291, 1307 (N.D. Ill. 1975) (Stevens, J.).

[77] Coleman v. Miller, 307 U.S. 438 (1939).

erroneously that states can exercise Tenth Amendment "reserved" power over the amendment process. Some have urged state legislatures and electorates to adopt state constitutional provisions, legislation, and interstate compacts to govern it. However, there is a very long line of cases holding that amendment powers derive solely from the Constitution, that Article V law is exclusively federal constitutional law, and that ordinary state (or federal) legislation cannot manipulate the process. Virtually without exception, the courts have invalidated efforts to use state law in that way.[78] These

---

[78] In chronological order, see *Herbring v. Brown*, 180 P. 328 (Or. 1919); *Barlotti v. Lyons*, 189 P.282 (Cal. 1920) (similar holding); *Opinion of the Justices*, 107 A. 673 (Me. 1919); Prior, 188 P. 727; Hawke I, 253 U.S. 221; Hawke II, 253 U.S. 231; *Leser v. Garnett*, 258 U.S. 130, 137 (1922) (Brandeis, J.); *State ex rel. Tate v. Sevier*, 333 Mo. 662, 62 S.W.2d 895 (1933), cert. denied 290 U.S. 679 (1933); Coleman, 307 U.S. 438; *State v. Hatch*, 526 P.2d 1369 (Mont. 1974); Dyer, 390 F. Supp. 1291; Opinion of the Justices to the Senate, 366 N.E.2d at 1228; *AFL-CIO v. Eu*, 86 P.2d 609, 620 (Cal. 1984), stay denied sub nom. *Uhler v. AFL-CIO*, 468 U.S. 1310 (1984); *State ex rel. Harper v. Waltermire*, 691 P.2d 826 (Mont. 1984), stay denied 469 U.S. 1301 (1984)' *Donovan v. Priest*, 326 Ark. 353, 931 S.W.2d 119 (1996), cert. denied 519 U.S. 1147 (1997); In re *Initiative Petition No. 264*, 930 P.2d 186 (Okla. 1996); *League of Women Voters v. Gwadosky*, 966 F. Supp. 52 (D. Me. 1997); *Morrissey v. State*, 951 P.2d 911 (Colo. 1998); *Barker v. Hazeltine*, 3 F. Supp. 2d 1088, 1093 (D.S.D. 1998); *Bramberg v. Jones*, 978 P.2d 1240 (Cal. 1999); *Miller v. Moore*, 169 F.3d 1119 (8th Cir. 1999).

See also Calzone v. Richard, (Mo. Cir. Ct. 2018), *available at* https://i2i.org/wp-content/uploads/2018-Calzone-v.-Richard-MO-CirCt.pdf ("The legislature was not exercising its power to enact laws when it approved [an Article V application], rather it was exercising authority granted under Article V of the United States Constitution. A state constitution may not add requirements to Article V's process for amending the federal constitution").Thus, *Dyer v. Blair*, 390 F. Supp. 1291 (N.D. Ill. 1975) (Stevens, J.) held that a requirement in the Illinois constitution requiring a three-fifths vote to ratify an amendment was not binding on the ratifying legislature. It follows that KAN. CONST. art. II, § 13, requiring a two-thirds vote of each entire house to apply or ratify, is not enforceable.

cases make it clear, moreover, that the application, ratification, proposal, and "Mode of Ratification" procedures all are governed by the same principles.[79]

Article V assemblies are not departments of the federal government, but they do exercise "federal functions."[80] In that capacity, Congress and state legislatures act as proposing or assenting bodies on behalf of the people rather than as legislatures.[81]

For a detailed examination of the constitutionality of one effort to control the amendment process through state law, see ROBERT G. NATELSON, IS THE "COMPACT FOR AMERICA" PLAN TO AMEND THE CONSTITUTION CONSTITUTIONAL? (Article V Information Center 2016), *available at* https://i2i.org/wp-content/uploads/2015/01/CFA-Report-final3a.pdf.

The same principle applies to federal law. Idaho v. Freeman, 529 F. Supp. 1107, 1127-28 (D. Idaho 1981), *judgment vacated as moot sub nom.* Carmen v. Idaho, 459 U.S. 809 (1982) ("In proposing or acting on a proposed constitutional amendment Congress is not acting pursuant to its 'ordinary' legislative powers found in article I but acts according to those powers granted under article V) (relying on Hollingsworth v. Virginia, 3 U.S. 376 (1798); *id.* at 1151 ("Thus, Congress, outside of the authority granted by article V, has no power to act with regard to an amendment, i.e., it does not retain any of its traditional authority vested in it by article I").

[79] *See supra* note 78; *see also* Spriggs v. Clark, 14 P.2d 667 (Wyo. 1932) (assuming that same rules apply to application as to ratification process).

[80] *Leser*, 258 U.S. at 137; State *ex rel.* Donnelly v. Myers, 186 N.E. 918 (Ohio 1933); *Sevier*, 62 S.W.2d 895.

[81] *Hawke I*, 253 U.S. 221; Hollingsworth v. Virginia, 3 U.S. (3 Dall.) 381 (1798); *Prior*, 188 P. 729; *see also Hawke II*, 253 U.S. 231; Dillon v. Gloss, 256 U.S. 368, 374 (1921) (stating that people assent to amendments through representative assemblies); *Sevier*, 62 S.W.2d 895; Calzone v. Richard, (Mo. Cir. Ct. 2018), *available at* https://i2i.org/wp-content/uploads/2018-Calzone-v.-Richard-MO-CirCt.pdf ("The legislature was not exercising its power to enact laws when it approved [an application for a convention], rather it was exercising authority granted under Article V of the United States Constitution").

The Constitution's grants of power to various assemblies (Congress, state legislatures, federal and state conventions) are as follows:[82]

- Authority to two thirds of each house of Congress to "propose" amendments.
- Authority to two thirds of the state legislatures to make "Application" for a convention for proposing amendments.
- Authority to Congress to "call" that convention.
- Authority to the convention "for proposing" amendments.
- Authority to Congress to decide whether ratification shall be by state legislatures or state conventions.
- If Congress selects the former method, authority to state legislatures to ratify or reject.
- If Congress selects the latter method, implied authority and a mandate to each state legislature to call a ratifying convention.
- Authority to three fourths of those conventions to ratify.
- Authority incidental to the foregoing, such as the power of all Article V assemblies to establish their own rules,[83] and the power of state legislatures to define the scope of their applications, to determine the mode for selecting commissioners (delegates), and to fix how state ratifying conventions are selected.

---

[82] For a slightly different formulation, see Natelson, *Rules, supra* note 21, at 702–03.

[83] *Dyer*, 390 F. Supp. at 1306 (referring to power of a legislature or convention operating under Article V to establish its own rules); Opinion of the Justices, 167 A. 176 (Me. 1933) (ratification conventions pass on the elections of their own members).

Additional information on both principal and incidental powers is found below.[84]

§ 3.7. Under Article V, a State "Legislature" Means the State's Representative Assembly, without Participation by the Governor or by Any Reserved Power of Initiative or Referendum.

Article V grants authority to legislatures and conventions as independent assemblies, not to branches of the federal or state governments. A state "Legislature," as Article V uses the term, means the state's law-making representative body, not the entire legislative power of the states.[85] The Supreme Court recently reaffirmed this while distinguishing the grants in Article V from those in the Constitution's Elections Clause, which does grant power to the general legislative power of the states.[86]

---

[84] *Infra* § 3.9.3.

[85] *Hawke I*, 253 U.S. 221; *Opinion of the Justices*, 107 A. 673; *Prior*, 188 P. 729; Decher v. Sec'y of State, 177 N.W. 288 (Mich. 1920); *see also Hawke II*, 253 U.S. 231; Idaho v. Freeman, 529 F. Supp. 1107 (D. Idaho 1981), *judgment vacated as moot sub nom*. Carmen v. Idaho, 459 U.S. 809 (1982); *Dyer*, 390 F. Supp. at 1306 (referring to power of a convention or legislature operating under Article V to establish its own rules). *See also* cases cited *supra* note 78.

[86] Ariz. State Legislature v. Ariz. Indep. Redistricting Comm'n, 135 S. Ct. 2652, 2668 (2015):

> [T]he meaning of the word 'legislature,' used several times in the Federal Constitution, differs according to the connection in which it is employed, depend[ent] upon the character of the function which that body in each instance is called upon to exercise." Thus "the Legislature" comprises the referendum and the Governor's veto in the context of regulating congressional elections. . . . In the context of ratifying constitutional amendments, in contrast, "the Legislature" has a different identity, one that excludes the referendum and the Governor's veto.
> (Internal citations omitted).

Thus, the President need not sign, and may not veto, congressional amendment proposals.[87] Similarly, state legislatures have authority to apply and ratify without gubernatorial intervention.[88] On the other hand, a gubernatorial signature should not invalidate the application.

Other methods, including initiative and referendum, may not displace the methods outlined in Article V, either directly or indirectly.[89] A referendum may not ratify in lieu of the state legislature[90] or state convention,[91] nor may initiatives, referenda, or state constitutional or

---

[87] Hollingsworth v. Virginia, 3 U.S. (3 Dall.) 381 (1798); *Opinion of the Justices*, 107 A. 673.

[88] Natelson, *Rules, supra* note 21, at 710–12; Opinion of the Justices to the Senate, 366 N.E.2d 1226 (Mass. 1977); Opinion of the Justices, 673 A.2d 693 (Me. 1996); Calzone v. Richard, (Mo. Cir. Ct. 2018), *available at* https://i2i.org/wp-content/uploads/2018-Calzone-v.-Richard-MO-CirCt.pdf.

[89] *Hawke I*, 253 U.S. 221; *Prior*, 188 P. 729; *see Hawke II*, 253 U.S. 231; *Sevier*, 62 S.W.2d 895; *see also* cases cited *supra* note 78. This is so, although references to the state legislature in other parts of the Constitution may include the referendum power. Smiley v. Holm, 285 U.S. 355 (1932) (stating that the constitutional meaning of "legislature" depends on the function, and that it can refer to a lawmaking, ratifying, electing, or consenting body; of course, it may also mean an applying body); Ohio *ex rel.* Davis v. Hildebrant, 241 U.S. 565 (1916) (construing the Times, Places and Manner Clause); State *ex rel.* Harper v. Waltermire, 691 P.2d 826 (Mont. 1984) (dicta).

The prohibition of initiatives and referenda is not changed by the holding in *Arizona State Legislature v. Arizona Independent Redistricting Commission*, 135 S. Ct. 2652, 2668 (2015). In that case, the Supreme Court upheld the use of voter initiative for an exercise of power delegated to state "Legislatures" by the Constitution's Elections Clause. This is because, as the Court makes clear, the Elections Clause delegation is to the states' general legislative authority. The Court also makes it clear that Article V's delegations to state "Legislatures," by contrast, are to those legislatures acting as independent assemblies. 135 S. Ct. at 2668.

[90] *Hawke I,* 253 U.S. 221; *see also Hawke II,* 253 U.S. 231; State *ex rel.* Donnelly v. Myers, 186 N.E. 918 (Ohio 1933); State v. Hatch, 526 P.2d 1369 (Mont. 1974).

[91] Opinion of the Justices, 167 A. 176 (Me. 1933).

legal provisions be employed to coerce the state legislature or other Article V assemblies.[92] *Within the scope of its legal authority*, a legislature or convention exercising Article V functions acts as an independent deliberative assembly at the ratification stage,[93] at the application stage,[94] and at the proposal stage.[95] In the words of Justice Brandeis, its function "transcends any limitations sought to be

---

[92] Gralike v. Cooke, 191 F.3d 911 (8th Cir. 1999), *aff'd on other grounds*, 531 U.S. 510 (2001); Miller v. Moore, 169 F.3d 1119 (8th Cir. 1999); Barker v. Hazeltine, 3 F. Supp. 2d 1088 (D.S.D. 1998); League of Women Voters v. Gwadosky, 966 F. Supp. 52 (D. Me. 1997); Donovan v. Priest, 931 S.W.2d 119 (Ark. 1996); Bramberg v. Jones, 978 P.2d 1240 (Cal. 1999); AFL-CIO v. Eu, 686 P.2d 609 (Cal. 1984); Morrissey v. State, 951 P.2d 911 (Colo. 1998); *Waltermire*, 691 P.2d 826 (dicta); *In re* Initiative Petition 364, 930 P.2d 186 (Okla. 1996). *But see* Opinion of the Justices, 148 So. 107 (Ala. 1933) (a state law may require convention delegates to vote in accordance with the results of a referendum). As the cases cited here demonstrate, the Alabama holding has been repudiated everywhere.

[93] *Opinion of the Justices*, 167 A. at 180.

[94] *Waltermire*, 691 P.2d 826 (rejecting attempt to use initiative process to force legislature to apply for convention); In re *Initiative Petition No. 264*, 930 P.2d 186 (same).

[95] *Donovan*, 931 S.W.2d 119; *see also Gralike*, 191 F.3d 911; *Miller*, 169 F.3d 1119; *Barker*, 3 F. Supp. 2d 1088; *Gwadosky*, 966 F. Supp. 52; *Bramberg*, 978 P.2d 1240; *Morrissey*, 951 P.2d 911; Opinion of the Justices, 673 A.2d 693 (Me. 1996); *Waltermire*, 691 P.2d 826 (dicta); In re *Initiative Petition 364*, 930 P.2d 186.

Both convention history and basic principles of agency law make clear that free decision making occurs only within the scope of legal authority. *See infra* § 3.8.3. For example, a convention called to ratify a prescribed amendment may not ratify others. A convention called to consider proposing amendments of a particular kind may not disregard its limits and propose unrelated amendments. This is such an elementary point of law, it is jarring to hear earnest claims to the contrary made by those peddling "runaway convention" claims. *See* Robert G. Natelson, *A Response to the Runaway Scenario*, http://articlevinfocenter.com/a-response-to-the-runaway-scenario/.

imposed by the people of a state."[96] A court will not countenance "an unconstitutional attempt effectively to remove the Article V power from legislators and place it in the hands of the people, thus substituting popular will for the will of the independent 'deliberative assemblage' ... envisioned by the Framers of the Constitution."[97] However, the courts do permit advisory referenda on Article V questions.[98]

To be sure, in the one case in which state conventions ratified a constitutional amendment, those conventions—although not actually coerced—acted de facto less as deliberative bodies than as registers of the popular will.[99] As ratification bodies, however, they were limited to a "yes" or "no" vote; a convention for proposing amendments is not.

Assemblies exercising functions under Article V enjoy powers incidental to those expressly granted by Article V.[100] Examples are the traditional prerogatives of legislatures and conventions to establish their own rules and elect their own officers. The rule barring coercion of an assembly operating under Article V surely should apply

---

[96] Leser v. Garnett, 258 U.S. 130, 137 (1922); *see also* Trombetta v. Florida, 353 F. Supp. 575 (M.D. Fla. 1973) (explaining that *Leser* struck down not just referenda but other state law efforts to control the Article V process, and holding that under *Leser* a state constitution may not impair a state legislature in its ratification function).

[97] *Miller*, 169 F.3d 1119.

[98] Kimble v. Swackhamer, 439 U.S. 1385 (1978) (Rehnquist, J.) (upholding advisory referendum); Simpson v. Cenarrusa, 944 P.2d 1372 (Idaho 1997).

[99] Everett Somerville Brown, *The Ratification of the Twenty-First Amendment*, 29 AM. POL. SCI. REV. 1005, 1017 (1935). Of course, ratifying convention delegates could have changed their positions during the deliberative process, just as many delegates did when considering whether to ratify the Constitution. There is no mechanism for recalling popularly-elected delegates as there is for recalling commissioners to a convention of the states.

[100] State *ex rel.* Tate v. Sevier, 62 S.W.2d 895 (Mo. 1933).

to that assembly's incidental powers.[101] Thus, federal laws and state laws and constitutions may not compel those assemblies to follow certain rules or submit to certain officers. By the same reasoning, Congress cannot employ its lawmaking power or its power to "call" to prescribe rules and procedures to a convention for proposing amendments. A court may, however, find that a legislature performing Article V functions has impliedly adopted a pre-existing rule.[102]

§ 3.8. The State Legislatures' Applications

§ 3.8.1. Background

In Founding-Era practice, a state legislature, a prior convention, or Congress could invite states to send commissioners to a federal convention. The invitation was a kind of application[103]—and might be denoted as such[104]—but it usually was labeled a *call*.

---

[101] Dyer v. Blair, 390 F. Supp. 1291, 1307-08 (N.D. Ill. 1975) (Stevens, J.):

> Article V identifies the body—either a legislature or a convention—which must ratify a proposed amendment. The act of ratification is an expression of consent to the amendment by that body. By what means that body shall decide to consent or not to consent is a matter for that body to determine for itself... We have concluded that article V delegates to the state legislatures—or the state conventions... the power to determine their own voting requirements.

[102] Dyer v. Blair, 390 F. Supp. 1291 (N.D. Ill. 1975) (Stevens, J.) (holding a state legislative voting rule not binding on, but impliedly accepted by, the legislature operating under Article V).

[103] *Supra* note 26 and accompanying text.

[104] For an example of the term "application" being used as a synonym for "call," see Natelson, *Conventions*, at 642 (reproducing a letter from the then-president of Massachusetts leading to the 1776–1777 Providence Convention).

The Constitution standardized both vocabulary and usage. Article V denotes a legislative notice to Congress as an application and provides that it may be issued only by a state legislature. Article V denotes the actual invitation as the call, and provides that it may be issued only by Congress. However, when two thirds of the states have applied on the same topic, Congress must call the convention to deal with that topic; Congress has no discretion in that matter.[105]

§ 3.8.2. What Is an Application and How Is It Adopted?

An application is a resolution of a state legislature (1) conditionally (2) authorizing and (3) directing Congress to call a convention on the topics listed in the application. It is *conditional* because it is subject to the condition of a sufficient number of other states applying for a convention on the same subject matter. It is an *authorization* because the process is a state-driven one, and Congress calls the convention as an agent for the states. It is a *direction* because once the condition is met, Congress is obliged to issue the call. An application may include statements of purpose (preambles or "whereas" clauses), but need not do so.

Article V grants power to make application to the state legislatures alone.[106] Neither the state constitution, state laws, nor normal legislative procedures are binding on the legislature when it acts under Article V.[107] If, however, the legislature does follow those laws and procedures, a court may rule that the legislature has assented impliedly to them.[108]

---

[105] THE FEDERALIST No. 85 (Alexander Hamilton); Tench Coxe, *A Pennsylvanian to the Convention of the State of New York*, Jun. 11, 1788, *reprinted in* 20 DOCUMENTARY HISTORY, *supra* note 57 1139, 1142–43 (Merrill Jensen, John P. Kaminsky, & Gaspare J. Saladino eds., 2009); Tench Coxe, *A Friend of Society and Liberty*, PA. GAZETTE, July 23, 1788, *reprinted in* 18 *id.* at 277, 284.

The necessary coincidence of the topics of the application and call is discussed *infra* § 3.9.6.

[106] *Supra* § 3.6.

[107] *Supra* § 3.7.

[108] Dyer v. Blair, 390 F. Supp. 1291 (N.D. Ill. 1975) (Stevens, J.).

Generally, bicameral state legislatures have adopted applications by individual chambers successively voting for the same resolution. However, the legislature may decide to vote on applications in a joint session. Similarly, at the time of consideration the applying legislature may opt to require a supermajority vote. In the absence of a decision to do so, action is by a majority of those present and voting, assuming a quorum.[109]

Applications may be adopted only pursuant to the grant of power in Article V. That Article grants power to apply only to the state legislature as an independent assembly, not to the state as such.[110] There is no formal role in the process for either the governor or for the people acting through initiative or referendum.[111] Purely advisory initiatives and referenda are permitted.[112]

State legislatures must transmit applications to Congress. State legislatures often provide for additional procedures, such as transmission to other states, but no such procedures are requisite for validity.[113] Generally, official state certification that an application has been passed precludes congressional and judicial investigation into the appropriateness of the process employed.[114]

---

[109] Ohio *ex rel.* Erkenbrecher v. Cox, 257 F. 334 (S.D. Ohio 1919) (dicta); *cf.* Rhode Island v. Palmer ("National Prohibition Cases"), 253 U.S. 350 (1920) (the requirement that "two thirds" of each house of Congress propose amendments means two thirds of the members present, assuming a quorum).

[110] *Supra* § 3.6.

[111] *Supra* § 3.7; *see also* Natelson, *Rules, supra* note 21, at 710–12.

[112] *Supra* § 3.7.

[113] United States *ex rel.* Widenmann v. Colby, 265 F. 998 (D.C. Cir. 1920), *aff'd*, 253 U.S. 350 (1921); *Cox*, 257 F. 334 (no requirement for validity of a ratification other than mentioned in Constitution).

[114] Leser v. Garnett, 258 U.S. 130 (1922) (holding that official notice by state legislatures that they had ratified bound the U.S. Secretary of State, whose certification was binding on the courts); Field v. Clark, 143 U.S. 649, 669–73 (1892) (holding that evidence that bill was signed by the Speaker of the House and President of the Senate and enrolled was conclusive that it was duly passed); Idaho v. Freeman, 529 F. Supp. 1107, 1150 (D. Idaho

§ 3.8.3. State Legislatures May Limit Their Applications to a Single Subject.

Political bodies normally have the power to define the scope of their resolutions. There should be, therefore, a presumption that a state legislature may apply for a convention to consider only certain topics rather than be required to apply only for a plenary or unlimited convention.[115] This has been the presumption upon which state lawmakers have proceeded: Only about twenty of the hundreds of state legislative applications issued since 1788 have been plenary.[116] Moreover, there has never been a serious movement to aggregate applications that do not overlap as to subject matter.[117]

Nevertheless, during the 1960s and 1970s, some legal writers (predominantly those opposing a convention) argued that all conventions must be plenary. A few even contended that limited applications were void by reason of their limits. These contentions were made on very slender evidence, and subsequent research has discredited them.[118] Founding-Era practice, upon which the Constitution's amendment convention was based, was to limit in advance the topic and scope of multi-government conventions.[119] Discussions from the Founding Era reveal a universal assumption that applications would

---

1981), *judgment vacated as moot sub nom.* Carmen v. Idaho, 459 U.S. 809 (1982); *Colby*, 265 F. 998; *Cox*, 257 F. 334.

[115] *Cf.* Opinion of the Justices to the Senate, 366 N.E.2d 1226 (Mass. 1977) (holding that a single-subject application is valid, although not dealing with the issue as to whether the limitation is enforceable).

[116] The Article V Library, article5library.org.

[117] Robert G. Natelson, *Counting to Two Thirds: How Close Are We to a Convention for Proposing Amendments to the Constitution?* 19 FED. SOC. REV. 51, 53 (2018) [hereinafter Natelson, *Counting*].

[118] *See, e.g.,* Michael B. Rappaport, *The Constitutionality of a Limited Convention: An Originalist Analysis,* 28 CONST. COMMENT. 53 (2012) [hereinafter Rappaport, *Limited Convention*]; *Stern, Reopening, supra* note 55.

[119] *See generally* Natelson, *Conventions, supra* note 2.

be made to promote amendments addressing prescribed problems.[120] The first application ever issued, that of Virginia in 1788,[121] while broad, was limited as to subject.[122] Indeed, the central purpose of the state application and convention procedure—to grant state legislatures parity with Congress in the proposal process—would be largely defeated unless those legislatures had the same power Congress enjoys to define an amendment's scope in advance.

It also follows from historical practice, not to mention common sense, that Congress should aggregate together towards the two-thirds threshold only those applications that address the same general topic.[123]

The limits on the ability of the convention to "run away"—that is, exceed the scope of the applications and call—are not within the present scope of this work. Suffice to say that no prior American inter-governmental conventions have been clear "runaways." There is a common myth—originating in an anti-federalist calumny—that the 1787 Constitutional Convention was called only to amend the Articles of Confederation, but that it "ran away" by proposing a new Constitution. This story is simply untrue.[124]

In any event, there are numerous and redundant legal checks on an Article V convention exceeding its authority.[125]

---

[120] Natelson, *Rules, supra* note 21, at 723–31; Rappaport, *Limited Convention, supra* note 118, at 83–89; Stern, *Reopening, supra* note 55, at 771.

[121] This application is substantially reproduced in Natelson, *Rules, supra* note 21, at 739, along with its unlimited New York counterpart.

[122] *Id.*, at 731–32.

[123] *Infra* § 3.9.6.

[124] Michael Farris, *Defying Conventional Wisdom: The Constitution Was Not the Product of a Runaway Convention*, 40 HARVARD J. L. & PUB. POL'Y 61 (2017). *See generally* Natelson, *Conventions, supra* note 2 and, on the Constitutional Convention, see *id.* at 674 and Natelson, *Rules, supra* note 21, at 719–23.

[125] ROBERT G. NATELSON, PROPOSING CONSTITUTIONAL AMENDMENTS BY A CONVENTION OF THE STATES: A HANDBOOK FOR STATE LAWMAKERS 17–18 (Am. Legislative Exch. Council, 3d ed. 2017), https://i2i.org/wp-content/uploads/2016-Article-V_FINAL_WEB-1.pdf; *see also* Rappaport,

§ 3.8.4. Application Format, Conditions, and Subject Matter

An application should be addressed to Congress. It should assert specifically and unequivocally that it is an application to Congress for a convention pursuant to Article V. The resolution should not merely request that Congress propose a particular amendment, nor should it merely request that Congress call a convention. An example of effective language is as follows:

> The legislature of the State of _____ hereby applies to Congress, under the provisions of Article V of the Constitution of the United States, for the calling of a convention of the states limited to proposing amendments to the Constitution of the United States that [here state general topic for convention].

Conditions on applications may or may not be valid, depending on the nature of the condition.[126] However, they are not recommended. Besides the fact that a court may declare a condition invalid, there is a risk that conflicting conditions among state applications otherwise covering the same subject may prevent Congress from aggregating them toward the two-thirds threshold. There is also the risk that conditions may be seen as coercing Congress or the convention in a manner not permitted by Article V.

As noted above, single subject applications are almost certainly valid and enforceable. The same cannot be said for applications that purport to dictate to the convention specific amendment wording. The courts and Congress may, with some justification, see them as invalid because they are inconsistent with historical practice and in-

---

Limited Convention, supra note 118, at 81–82; Stern, *Reopening, supra* note 55, at 781–87. For a detailed response to "runaway" alarmism, see Robert G. Natelson, *A Response to the Runaway Scenario*, http://articlevinfocenter.com/a-response-to-the-runaway-scenario/.

[126] Conditional applications and calls were recognized during the Founding Era. *See, e.g.*, Natelson, *Conventions, supra* note 2, at 661–62; *cf.* Idaho v. Freeman, 529 F. Supp. 1107, 1154 (D. Idaho 1981), *judgment vacated as moot sub nom.* Carmen v. Idaho, 459 U.S. 809 (1982) (declining to rule on the issue while criticizing the claim that conditions are void or void an application).

terfere with the normal discretion afforded to a proposal convention.[127] To the extent that specific wording varies among applications, it also will impede congressional aggregation toward the two-thirds threshold. Although some scholars believe applications mandating specific wording are constitutionally permissible, legal issues and potential aggregation problems place them in doubt.

§ 3.8.5. State Legislatures May Rescind Applications.

Some have argued that states cannot rescind applications, and that once adopted an application continues in effect forever, unless a convention is called. In part, this is based on judicial deference to congressional suggestions that a *ratification* cannot be rescinded.[128] However, the position that applications cannot be rescinded is contrary to the principles of agency the Founders incorporated into the process. An application is a deputation from the state legislature to Congress to call a convention. Just as one may withdraw authority from an agent before the interest of a third party vests, so may the state legislature withdraw authority from Congress before the two-thirds threshold is reached.[129]

This theoretical conclusion is consistent with traditional multi-government convention practice. The power of a state to rescind its resolutions, offers, and ratifications was well-established by the time Article V was adopted, ending only when the culmination of a joint process was reached. The historical record contains specific examples of rescission of convention applications and calls.[130]

---

[127] See *supra* § 3.7 for the deliberative nature of Article V assemblies.

[128] Coleman v. Miller, 307 U.S. 438 (1939) (stating that congressional decisions against rescission will be respected); Opinion of the Justices, 107 A. 673 (Me. 1919). *But see Freeman*, 529 F. Supp. at 1141 (noting that Congress has not come to a definitive conclusion on rescission of ratifications).

[129] Natelson, *Rules, supra* note 21, at 712; *Freeman*, 529 F. Supp. 1107 (holding that ratifications can be rescinded until the three-fourths minimum is reached).

[130] *E.g.*, Natelson, *Conventions, supra* note 2, at 666.

§ 3.8.6. Unrescinded Applications Do Not Grow "Stale" with the Passage of Time.[131]

Some have argued that applications automatically become "stale" after an unspecified period of time, and no longer count toward a two-thirds majority. However, there is no evidence from the Founding Era or from other American practice implying that applications become stale automatically or that Congress can declare them to be so. On the contrary, during the constitutional debates, participants noted with approval the Constitution's general lack of time requirements in the amendment process. Moreover, the ministerial nature of the congressional duty to call a convention and Congress's role as the agent for those legislatures in this process, suggests the opposite. Time limits are for principals, not agents, to impose. Therefore, if a state legislature believes its application to be stale, that legislature may rescind it.

The argument that applications can become stale traditionally has been buttressed by a 1921 Supreme Court case, *Dillon v. Gloss*,[132] which suggested that *ratifications*, to be valid, must be issued within a reasonable time of each other. Of course a rule pertaining to ratifications does not necessarily pertain to applications, and this was certainly true of the rationale behind the *Dillon* court's statement.[133] Moreover, subsequent events have removed the prop for that statement, even as to ratifications: The *Dillon* language was predicated upon the court's doubt that proposed amendments could survive a very long ratification period.[134] That doubt was dispelled, however, by the universally recognized adoption of the Twenty-

---

[131] This section is based largely on Natelson, *Rules, supra* note 21, at 712–14, but also includes new information.

[132] 256 U.S. 368 (1921).

[133] The "staleness" discussion in *Dillon* was based partly on presumed congressional power to set ratification time limits as an incident of its power to choose one of two "Mode[s] of Ratification." However, congressional authority to call a convention for proposing amendments is narrower than its authority over ratification: The latter is partly discretionary, the former is ministerial.

[134] *Dillon*, 256 U.S. at 375.

Seventh Amendment based on ratifications stretching over two centuries. In any event, the courts have edged away from the "staleness" rationale of *Dillon*.[135]

An additional factor against the "staleness" contention is that there is no appropriate umpire—other than the issuing state legislature—to judge the issue. It is not resolvable by the courts for lack of "judicially manageable standards,"[136] and for Congress to judge would be to invite abuse by interjecting that body into a process designed to bypass it. Thus, in the final analysis, the only proper judge of whether an application is fresh or stale is the legislature that adopted it. Any time a legislature deems an application (or ratification) to be outdated, the legislature may rescind it, as many have done.

---

[135] *Dillon* upheld the limit in the Eighteenth Amendment as incidental to the power to fix the mode of ratification, but the text of the amendment indicates that the limit was part of the original proposal itself. *See* United States v. Thibault, 47 F.2d 169, 169 (2d Cir. 1931) (reproducing the amendment's text). Since *Dillon*, the courts have corrected the basis on which the congressionally imposed seven-year ratification limit was justified. Thus, in *Coleman v. Miller*, 307 U.S. 438, 454 (1939) the Court stated that "[w]e have held that the Congress *in proposing an amendment* may fix a reasonable time for ratification." (Emphasis added); *see also* United States v. Gugel, 119 F. Supp. 897, 900 (E.D. Ky. 1954) (stating that time for ratification is not important "unless a period of limitation is fixed by the Congress *in the act submitting the amendment to the states*"—that is, in the proposal). In *Idaho v. Freeman*, 529 F. Supp. 1107, 1153 (D. Idaho 1981), *judgment vacated as moot sub nom. Carmen v. Idaho*, 459 U.S. 809 (1982), the court reported the original *Dillon* rationale, but noted that the time period in the proposed amendment before it was part of the congressional proposal itself.

[136] *Coleman*, 307 U.S. 438 (holding that there are no judicial standards for determining what time is reasonable); Dyer v. Blair, 390 F. Supp. 1291 (N.D. Ill. 1975) (Stevens, J.).

§ 3.9. The Congressional Role in Calling the Convention

§ 3.9.1. The Meaning of "Call"

Article V provides that "The Congress . . . on the Application of the Legislatures of two thirds of the several states, shall call a Convention for proposing Amendments. . . ." The following material discusses what it means for Congress to "call" a convention, the content of a call, the powers Congress enjoys as incidental to calling, and when Congress must issue a call.

The courts tell us that the terms of Article V are defined by historical usage.[137] That usage enables us to determine what it means for Congress to "call" a convention of the states.[138] Between 1677 and Independence in 1776, American colonies met in convention at least twenty times. From 1776 through 1787, the newly independent states met in convention eleven times, including general conventions[139] in Philadelphia in 1780 and 1787. Precipitating each gathering was an invitation to meet. Some invitations were issued by the Continental Congress or by prior conventions, but most came from individual states seeking to meet with other states. For example, the Constitutional Convention was not, as commonly believed, the product of a congressional resolution, but the result of an invitation extended by the Virginia legislature on December 1, 1786.[140]

---

[137] *Supra* § 3.5.

[138] For the characterization, by the Founding Generation and by the Supreme Court, of an Article V convention as a "convention of the states," see *supra* §§ 3.1 & 3.2.4.

[139] *Supra* § 3.1 (distinguishing between partial and general conventions). This survey of historical practice draws on Natelson, *Conventions, supra* note 2; see also *List of Conventions of States and Colonies in American History*, http://articlevinfocenter.com/list-conventions-states-colonies-american-history/.

[140] Article V Information Center, *Who Called the Constitutional Convention? Answer: The Commonwealth of Virginia*, http://articlevinfocenter.com/who-called-the-constitutional-convention-answer-the-commonwealth-of-virginia/; Michael Farris, *Defying Conven-*

In the parlance of the time, an *application* was merely an address, and to *apply* to another was to address him or her. An invitation to a convention was a kind of application, therefore, and sometimes was referred to such. Another common term for this special form of application was *call*.

In 1785, Massachusetts unsuccessfully asked Congress to issue a call, and referred to its own request as an "application."[141] In framing Article V, the drafters left most existing practices in place, but they tried to clarify uncertainties and standardize variations.[142] They decided to employ the word "application" as Massachusetts had in 1785—meaning a document preliminary to a call. Thus, in the vocabulary of Article V, the triggering legislative resolutions were to be "applications" and the invitation was to be the "call." The submission of applications from two thirds of the states would render the call mandatory rather than merely recommendatory, and Congress would serve as the common calling entity.

§ 3.9.2. Contents of the Call

The courts tell us that Article V terminology is defined by historical usage.[143] By examining calls from Founding-Era multi-state conventions, we can determine the contents of an Article V call.[144]

Entirely typical is the 1777 call by the Continental Congress for two multi-state conventions to deal with the problem of inflation during the Revolutionary War. Congress asked that one convention take place in York Town, Pennsylvania and another occur in Charleston, South Carolina. The call for both was as follows:

> That, for this purpose, it be recommended to the legislatures, or, in their recess, to the executive powers of the States of New

---

tional Wisdom: The Constitution Was Not the Product of a Runaway Convention, 40 HARVARD J. L. & PUB. POL'Y 61 (2017).

[141] *See* Natelson, *Conventions, supra* note 2, at 666–67.

[142] *Id.* at 689–90.

[143] *Supra* § 3.5.

[144] Natelson, *Conventions, supra* note 2, contains more than a dozen Founding-Era calls.

York, New Jersey, Pensylvania [*sic*], Delaware, Maryland, and Virginia, to appoint commissioners to meet at York town, in Pensylvania, on the 3d Monday in March next, to consider of, and form a system of regulation adapted to those States, to be laid before the respective legislatures of each State, for their approbation:

That, for the like purpose, it be recommended to the legislatures, or executive powers in the recess of the legislatures of the States of North Carolina, South Carolina, and Georgia, to appoint commissioners to meet at Charlestown [*sic*], in South Carolina, on the first Monday in May next. . . .[145]

This call designated the states invited and fixed the time, place, and purpose of the meeting. Some other Founding-Era calls included provisions for notifying the invitees and, if the calling agency was a state, that state's designation of its own commissioners. (Illustrative of the latter practice is the December 1, 1786 Virginia legislation that called the Constitutional Convention.)[146] However, Founding-Era calls did not try to control the composition, rules, or conduct of the convention beyond designating time, place, and purpose. To reassure readers on this point, the text of several calls is reproduced below in Section 4.6.

Massachusetts made two efforts to go beyond the "time, place, and purpose" trilogy, but both were unsuccessful. The call to the 1765 Stamp Act Congress asked that state delegations be "Committees" from the *lower houses* of the various colonies. The reason was that most of the colonial upper houses were controlled, directly or indirectly, by the Crown. Several colonies failed to follow this prescription, and the convention seated each committee regardless of how selected.[147] Massachusetts' 1783 invitation for a

---

[145] *Id.* at 645.

[146] *See infra* § 4.6 (reproducing the Virginia call).

[147] C.A. WESLAGER, THE STAMP ACT CONGRESS (1976). The call itself is reproduced *id.* at 181–82. The New York commissioners were selected by the legislature's committee of correspondence, *id.* at 81, and the Delaware commissioners by a rump of former legislators. *Id.* at 93–99.

tax convention at Hartford sought to dictate that the convention act, "by the majority of the delegates so to be convened" rather than by a majority of states. However, two of the four states invited refused to participate, and Massachusetts was forced to rescind.[148] Thus, by the time the Constitution was written, established custom held that a convention call could prescribe to the states and the convention no more than the "time, place, and purpose" trilogy.

One may contrast this trilogy with the "time, place, and manner" language common in Founding-Era election law, and appearing in the Constitution itself.[149] Both phrases share the terms "time" and "place," but the *manner* of election differs from the *purpose* of a convention. When a Founding-Era legislature determined the "manner of election," it described the means: the rules by which electors were to make their choices.[150] The "purpose," on the other hand, described the goal of the process rather than the means. In multi-state convention practice, the means—the rules of decision—were left to the participants: the state legislatures and their respective representatives in convention assembled.

In 1861, Virginia called the Washington Conference Convention to try to craft a compromise to avoid the Civil War. Although this

---

One might read the call of Connecticut for the 1780 Boston convention as seeking to prescribe how some of the other states appointed their commissioners. However, that language probably represents merely an understanding of which state legislatures were in session and which ones were in recess. In any event, the result was the same as it was for the Stamp Act Congress: states appointed commissioners as they pleased, and all were seated. The call for the 1780 Boston Convention is found in PROCEEDINGS OF A CONVENTION OF DELEGATES FROM SEVERAL OF THE NEW-ENGLAND STATES, HELD AT BOSTON, AUGUST 3–9, 1780, at 53–55 (Franklin B. Hough ed., 1867), and discussed in Natelson, *Conventions, supra* note 2, at 659–60.

[148] Natelson, *Conventions, supra* note 2, at 666.

[149] U.S. CONST. art. I, § 4, cl. 4 ("Times, Places and Manner of holding Elections").

[150] Robert G. Natelson, *The Original Scope of the Congressional Power to Regulate Elections*, 13 U. PA. J. CONST. L. 1 (2010).

general convention was not called under Article V, in every other respect it was a twin of an Article V convention for proposing amendments.[151] The operative language of the call was as follows:

> Resolved, That on behalf of the commonweath [sic] of Virginia, an invitation is hereby extended to all such States, whether slaveholding or non-slaveholding, as are willing to unite with Virginia in an earnest effort to *adjust the present unhappy controversies*, in the spirit in which the Constitution was originally formed, and consistently with its principles, so as to afford to the people of the slaveholding States adequate guarantees for the security of their rights, to appoint commissioners to meet on the *fourth day of February next*, in the *City of Washington*, similar commisioners [sic] appointed by Virginia, to consider, and if practicable, agree upon some suitable adjustment.[152]

As the italicized language indicates: time, place, and purpose.

§ 3.9.3. Congressional Powers Incidental to the Call

Unlike the Articles of Confederation, the Constitution conveyed powers incidental to those enumerated. The incidental power doctrine is discussed above in Section 3.5. Essentially, it holds that when construing enumerated powers, one should infer certain unlisted subordinate powers—specifically those tied to the enumerated powers by custom or reasonable necessity. The doctrine is a way of fully effectuating the intent of those who adopted an instrument.

Because incidental powers are always subordinate, they cannot be as important as their principals[153]—a point reinforced by Chief Justice John Roberts in a 2012 case.[154] Moreover, as Chief Justice John Marshall observed, authority incidental to a constitutional grant

---

[151] See *infra* § 3.14.2 for an explanation of the relative importance of the Washington Conference Convention.

[152] WASHINGTON CONFERENCE REPORT, *supra* note 35, at 9 (emphasis added).

[153] See *supra* § 3.5.

[154] Nat'l Fed'n of Indep. Bus. v. Sebelius, 567 U.S. 519, 599-62 (2012).

must be consistent with the "spirit" of the Constitution.[155] Thus, a power that subverts a purpose of the express grant cannot be incidental to it.

Article V grants enumerated powers to Congress, to potential amendments conventions, to state legislatures, and to potential state ratifying conventions. In accordance with the courts' direction that we look to historical practice,[156] certain historical incidents follow these grants. Thus, state legislatures enjoy incidental authority to define the subject of their applications and to appoint and instruct their commissioners. State legislatures enjoy the incidental power of arranging for ratifying conventions. Conventions may adopt their own rules.[157]

Historical practice tells us that setting the initial time and place of meeting and describing the subject matter is part of the "call."[158] Certainly Congress, while serving for this purpose as an agent of the state legislatures, may count the number of applications addressing any one topic or group of topics.[159] Congress may provide a place to store applications and keep related records, to define the convention's subjects in the way most faithful to the applications, to respond to state requests for relevant information, and to notify the appropriate state officials of the call.[160]

---

[155] McCulloch v. Maryland, 17 U.S. 316, 421 (1819) (stating that means must "consist with the letter and spirit of the constitution").

[156] *See supra* § 3.5.

[157] *See supra* § 3.5; *infra* § 3.14.

[158] *See supra* § 3.9.2.

[159] *See infra* § 3.9.6 (discussing how Congress counts applications).

[160] In *Dillon v. Gloss*, 256 U.S. 368 (1921), the Supreme Court seemed to take a more expansive view of Congress's incidental powers under Article V by upholding its time limit for ratification in the Eighteenth Amendment as incidental to the power to fix the mode of ratification. However, the text of the amendment indicates that the limit was part of the original proposal itself. *See* United States v. Thibault, 47 F.2d 169, 169 (2d Cir. 1931) (reproducing the amendment's text). Since *Dillon*, the courts have corrected the basis on which the congressionally imposed seven-year ratification limit was justified. Thus, in *Coleman v. Miller*, 307 U.S. 438, 454 (1939) the

On the other hand, Congress's authority incidental to the call is restricted. There are at least three reasons for so concluding. First, historically a call's prescriptions for a convention were limited to time, place, and purpose.[161] Second, incidental powers may not subvert the purpose of a grant. The overriding purpose of the state application and convention procedure is to bypass Congress.[162] If Congress could structure the convention, this would largely defeat its overriding purpose. Third, other actors in the process enjoy incidental authority as well, so Congress may not do anything to intrude upon that authority. If Congress were to dictate to state legislatures how select commissioners, then Congress would invade the incidental authority of state legislatures. If Congress were to set rules for the convention, it would intrude on the convention's incidental authority to adopt its own rules.

§ 3.9.4. The Necessary and Proper Clause Does Not Authorize Congress to Structure the Convention.

The Necessary and Proper Clause appears in Article I, Section 8 at the end of an (incomplete) list of congressional powers. It reads:

Court stated that "[w]e have held that the Congress *in proposing an amendment* may fix a reasonable time for ratification." (Emphasis added); *see also* United States v. Gugel, 119 F. Supp. 897, 900 (E.D. Ky. 1954) (stating that the time of ratification is not important "unless a period of limitation is fixed by the Congress *in the act submitting the amendment to the states*"—that is, in the proposal) (emphasis added). In *Idaho v. Freeman*, 529 F. Supp. 1107, 1153 (D. Idaho 1981), judgment vacated as moot sub nom. *Carmen v. Idaho*, 459 U.S. 809 (1982), the court reported the original *Dillon* rationale, but noted that the time period in the proposed amendment was part of the congressional proposal itself.

In any event, the scope of powers incidental to selecting the mode of ratification does not determine the scope of powers incidental to calling a convention, particularly since the purpose of the convention is to bypass Congress.

[161] *See supra* § 3.9.2.
[162] *See supra* § 3.3.

The Congress shall have Power ... To make all Laws which shall be necessary and proper for carrying into Execution the foregoing Powers, and all other Powers vested by this Constitution in the Government of the United States, or in any Department or Officer thereof.[163]

In 1963, Yale University law professor Charles Black wrote an article fiercely opposing the application and convention procedure.[164] Without doing much research on the matter, Black argued that upon receipt of sufficient applications, Congress could employ the Necessary and Proper Clause to structure the convention as it pleased.[165] In 1967 and twice thereafter, Senator Sam Ervin (D–N.C.), who professed himself a friend to the process, introduced legislation by which Congress would have fixed the method by which states adopt applications, prescribed how long they would last, dictated the procedure for selecting delegates, apportioned those delegates among the states, and imposed rules upon the convention, including the margin of votes necessary for making decisions.[166] From time to time, members of Congress have introduced similar bills. None has passed.[167]

Reliance on the Necessary and Proper Clause to justify bills of this kind assumes a certain stupidity on the part of the Constitution's Framers: That is, it assumes that the Framers drafted the Necessary and Proper Clause broadly enough to enable Congress to control a process designed to circumvent itself. In fact, the Framers did no such thing. Such bills are unconstitutional for at least three reasons.

---

[163] U.S. CONST. art. I, § 8, cl. 18.

[164] Charles L. Black, Jr., *The Proposed Amendment of Article V: A Threatened Disaster*, 72 YALE L.J. 957 (1963).

[165] Professor Black may have been encouraged by the Supreme Court's use of the Clause in expanding the Commerce Power. However, the Court generally has not applied the Clause that way in other contexts.

[166] Sam J. Ervin, Jr., *Proposed Legislation to Implement the Convention Method of Amending the Constitution*, 66 MICH. L. REV. 875 (1967).

[167] *See* THOMAS H. NEALE, THE ARTICLE V CONVENTION TO PROPOSE CONSTITUTIONAL AMENDMENTS: CONTEMPORARY ISSUES FOR CONGRESS (Cong. Research Serv., Mar. 7, 2014) (discussing these efforts).

First, the Necessary and Proper Clause does not apply to Article V. By its terms, it applies only to powers listed in Article I, Section 8 (which are not pertinent to Article V) and to powers vested (1) in the "Government of the United States" and (2) in "Departments" and "Officers" of that government.

As pointed out earlier, when Congress, state legislatures, and conventions act in the amendment process, they do so not as "Department[s]" of government, but as ad hoc assemblies.[168] Indeed, Article V is only one of several provisions in the Constitution that delegates tasks to persons or entities that do not act as agents of the U.S. Government. For example, Article I, Section 2 confers authority on state governors to issue writs of election to fill vacancies in the House of Representatives. Article I, Section 4 grants to the state legislative authorities the power to regulate congressional elections.[169] Before the Seventeenth Amendment, Article I, Section 3 empowered state legislatures to elect U.S. Senators. Article II, Section 1, coupled with the Twelfth Amendment, empowers the Electoral College to select the President. By its wording, the Necessary and Proper Clause does not extend to such independent actors.

To be sure, all of these persons and entities receive their authority from the Constitution and therefore are said to exercise "federal functions."[170] But exercise of a federal function does not render an independent actor part of, or an agent of, the U.S. Government.[171]

For this reason the Necessary and Proper Clause does not encompass the independent assemblies empowered by Article V,

---

[168] *Supra* §§ 3.6, 3.7.

[169] Ariz. State Legislature v. Ariz. Indep. Redistricting Comm'n, 135 S. Ct. 2652 (2015) (so noting, and distinguishing this power from the grant under Article V to state legislatures acting alone).

[170] *Supra* § 3.6; *see also* Ray v. Blair, 343 U.S. 214 (1952).

[171] *Ray*, 343 U.S. at 224–25 ("The presidential electors exercise a federal function in balloting for President and Vice-President but they are not federal officers or agents any more than the state elector who votes for congressmen. They act by authority of the state that in turn receives its authority from the federal constitution.").

even if, like Congress, they serve as part of government when acting in other capacities.[172]

Second, even if the Necessary and Proper Clause did encompass those assemblies, the Clause would not be broad enough to enable Congress to structure the convention. The Necessary and Proper Clause does not actually bestow any authority: It is a rule of interpretation designed to tell the reader that, unlike the Articles of Confederation, the Constitution conveys incidental powers to Congress.[173] Yet powers incidental to the call are quite limited.[174] Indeed, it could hardly be otherwise. The Ervin bills would have changed a state-driven process into one in which Congress intruded at the application stage and completely muscled out the state legislatures at the convention stage. No power may be incidental to an express provision that contradicts the basic purpose of its principal.[175]

Third, a line of twentieth century cases holds that government legislation cannot control the amendment process.[176]

---

[172] The non-applicability of the Necessary and Proper Clause helps explains why the Times, Places and Manner Clause (also called the Elections Clause) includes a specific term permitting Congress to act in the area. U.S. Const., art. I, § 4, cl. 1.

Another grant of power to Congress to act in an independent capacity—that is, outside its normal role as the legislature of the U.S. Government—is the Twelfth Amendment, which provides for the Senate and House of Representatives to serve as witnesses to the count of electoral votes in presidential elections.

[173] *See generally* Robert G. Natelson, *The Framing and Adoption of the Necessary and Proper Clause*, in GARY LAWSON, GEOFFREY P. MILLER, ROBERT G. NATELSON & GUY I. SEIDMAN, THE ORIGINS OF THE NECESSARY AND PROPER CLAUSE 84, 97–101 (2010) (discussing the adoption and meaning of the Clause); Nat'l Fed'n of Indep. Bus. v. Sebelius, 567 U.S. 519, 599 (2012) (quoting James Madison for the proposition that "the Clause is 'merely a declaration, for the removal of all uncertainty, that the means of carrying into execution those [powers] otherwise granted are included in the grant.'") (alteration in original).

[174] *Supra* § 3.9.3.
[175] *Supra* § 3.9.3.
[176] *Supra* note 78.

Such considerations strongly suggest that the courts would not permit Congress to interfere in the way contemplated by the Ervin bills. However, history tells us that litigation on the subject is unlikely. When Congress designated state conventions as the ratifying mechanism for the Twenty-First Amendment, some people suggested that Congress structure the ratifying conventions. Amid widespread objection that this was outside congressional authority or at least impractical, Congress left the task to the states, which managed the chore themselves.[177] This precedent, coupled with Congress's repeated failure over several decades to adopt the Ervin bills or comparable measures, suggests that the states will be left free to constitute an amendments convention as they choose.

§ 3.9.5. If Thirty-Four Applications on the Same Subject Are Received, the Call Is Mandatory.

The Constitution provides that Congress "shall call" an amendments convention on application by two thirds of the states (currently thirty-four). The language is obviously mandatory, and several leading Founders specifically represented it as such.[178] Historical usage informs us that an application or call can limit the subject matter of the proposed gathering: Virtually all applications and calls, before and during the Founding Era, had done so. Applications or calls for a convention dealing with one topic have never been treated together with applications or calls for a convention on another topic. For example, in 1786 there were simultaneous calls for a commercial convention and a navigation convention, but no one thought of aggregating them.[179] Similarly, in the early twentieth century there was no

---

[177] Everett Somerville Brown, *The Ratification of the Twenty-First Amendment*, 29 AM. POL. SCI. REV. 1005 (1935).

[178] Quotations are collected in Natelson, *Rules, supra* note 21, at 734–35 & nn.275–80). *See also* Tench Coxe, *A Pennsylvanian to the Convention of the State of New York*, Jun. 11, 1788, reprinted in 20 DOCUMENTARY HISTORY, *supra* note 57, at 1139, 1142–43.

[179] The Navigation Convention was to be a meeting of Pennsylvania, Delaware, and Maryland to discuss a canal and improvements in the water-

suggestion that applications for direct election of Senators should be aggregated with any of the numerous applications extant on other topics.[180] Thus, before Congress is obliged to call a convention, there must be thirty-four applications that overlap as to subject. The kind of overlap required is examined below in Section 3.9.6.

We normally think of Congress and state legislatures as discharging legislative functions, the President as discharging executive functions, and the courts as discharging judicial functions. As every lawyer knows, the Constitution's separation of powers is not always so neat. The President's veto is an exercise of legislative power. The Senate's review of his nominations is executive. Congressional impeachment proceedings are judicial. The powers exercised under Article V are *sui generis*.

The structure of the Constitution implies—and the courts tell us directly—that when Congress, other legislatures, and conventions operate under Article V, they discharge functions different from their usual roles, and that they serve as ad hoc agencies rather than as branches or departments of their respective governments.[181] When Congress proposes amendments or chooses a mode of ratification, it acts as an agent of the people rather than of the federal government,[182] just as a state legislature ratifying an amendment

---

ways leading to Philadelphia and Baltimore. It never met. The Annapolis Commercial Convention met in 1786, and issued a sort of application recommending to the governments of the states represented at the convention that they call the Constitutional Convention. On the Navigation Convention, see Natelson, *Conventions, supra* note 2, at 668–70.

[180] *Natelson, Counting, supra* note 117, at 53.

[181] *Supra* § 3.6.

[182] United States v. Sprague, 282 U.S. 716, 733 (1931); Idaho v. Freeman, 529 F. Supp. 1107, 1127-28 (D. Idaho 1981), *judgment vacated as moot sub nom.* Carmen v. Idaho, 459 U.S. 809 (1982) ("In proposing or acting on a proposed constitutional amendment Congress is not acting pursuant to its 'ordinary' legislative powers found in article I but acts according to those powers granted under article V) (relying on Hollingsworth v. Virginia, 3 U.S. 376 (1798); *id.* at 1151 ("Thus, Congress, outside of the authority granted by article V, has no power to act with regard to an amend-

serves as an agent of the people rather than as a branch of state government.

The Framers selected Congress to issue the call because it was a convenient central entity. The mandatory duty to call is clearly not a legislative function, but an executive one. It is not exercised on behalf of the federal government, but on behalf of the applying state legislatures. It is, moreover, ministerial in nature, and therefore should be enforceable judicially.[183] In other words, if Congress refuses to undertake its constitutional obligation, judicial relief—such as mandamus, a declaratory judgment, or an injunction—can compel it to do so.[184]

§ 3.9.6. Counting Applications

Article V provides that "The Congress ... on the Application of the Legislatures of two thirds of the several States, shall call a Convention for proposing Amendments." As Section 3.9.5 pointed out, Founding-Era evidence demonstrates that when "two thirds of the several States" apply, the duty to call arises only when they apply on the same general subjects.

To be sure, state applications are seldom identical. Congress will need to judge which applications should be aggregated. This is not inconsistent with the ministerial, mandatory nature of the congressional task, since even ministerial duties may call for exercise of

---

ment, i.e., it does not retain any of its traditional authority vested in it by article I").

[183] Ministerial duties and constitutional rules, even on Congress, are enforceable by the courts. *Cf.* Powell v. McCormick, 395 U.S. 486 (1969) (issuing a declaratory judgment for reinstatement of a member of Congress denied his seat); Roberts v. United States, 176 U.S. 222 (1900) (holding that threshold discretion as to construction of law does not alter ministerial nature of the duties).

[184] Absolute refusal by both Congress and the courts to issue, or require the issuance, of the mandated call would, of course, be unconstitutional behavior, and presumably would require an extra-constitutional response. For example, the states might call a plenipotentiary convention outside Article V. Extra-constitutional responses are not within the scope of this treatise.

threshold discretion.[185] But because the duty to call is mandatory and because the application and convention process is designed to bypass Congress, its exercise of discretion should be subject to heightened judicial scrutiny. This conclusion is strengthened by the fact that a refusal increases congressional authority, thereby creating a conflict of interest.

So long as thirty-four applications, however worded, agree that the convention is to consider a particular subject and do not include governing phrases fundamentally inconsistent with each other, the count may be easy. Aggregation may be facilitated by a recent trend (first suggested by this author) by which an applying legislature provides explicitly that its own applications should be aggregated with designated applications from other states.

In this area, history argues that flexibility is appropriate and that hyper-technical readings are not. Founding-Era resolutions calling conventions and empowering commissioners almost never matched identically—but many conventions were held.[186]

Thus, an application calling for an amendment limiting "outlays" to expected revenue surely should be counted with an application for an amendment limiting "appropriations" to expected revenue. These, in turn should be aggregated with applications calling merely for a convention to consider a "balanced budget amendment."

More difficult problems arise in four separate situations:

1. All applications seem to address the same subject, but some are inherently inconsistent with others.

2. Some applications prescribe a convention addressing Subject A while others prescribe a convention addressing both Subject A and unrelated Subject B.

3. Some applications prescribe a convention addressing Subject A (e.g., "a balanced budget amendment") while others demand one addressing Subject X, where Subject X encom-

---

[185] *Roberts,* 176 U.S. 222 (holding that threshold discretion as to construction of law does not alter ministerial nature of the duties).

[186] *See generally* Natelson, *Conventions, supra* note 2.

passes Subject A (e.g., "fiscal restraints on the federal government").

4. Some applications prescribe a convention addressing Subject A and others call for a plenary convention—one unlimited as to topic.

There is no direct judicial authority interpreting the Constitution on these points. We do know, however, that the Founders expected the document to be interpreted in the larger common law context, and that in interpreting the document themselves they freely resorted to analogies from both private and public law.[187]

In this instance, the closest analogue may be the law of contracts. Nearly all the Founders were social contractarians, and they frequently referred to the Constitution as a "compact."[188] The application process itself is closely akin to the kind of group offer and acceptance that leads to such legal relationships as partnerships and joint ventures. Like offers, applications may be rescinded. Like offers, they become binding on the parties when the conditions for

---

[187] For example, during the ratification process, James Iredell, a leading North Carolina lawyer and judge and subsequently associate justice of the Supreme Court, likened the Constitution's scheme of enumerated powers to a "great power of attorney," 4 THE DEBATES IN THE SEVERAL STATE CONVENTIONS OF THE ADOPTION OF THE FEDERAL CONSTITUTION 148–49, (Jonathan Elliot ed., 2d ed. 1827) [hereinafter ELLIOT'S DEBATES], while Edmund Pendleton explained the Constitution's delegation of powers by referring to (a) conveyance of a term of years, (b) conveyance of a fee tail or life estate, (c) conveyance of a fee simple, and (d) agency. Letter from Edmund Pendleton to Richard Henry Lee (Jun. 14, 1788), *reprinted in* 10 DOCUMENTARY HISTORY, *supra* note 57, at 1625–26 (Merrill Jensen et al. eds., 1976).

[188] The examples are many. *See, e.g.*, 3 ELLIOT'S DEBATES, *supra* note 186, at 384, 445, 591 (quoting Patrick Henry, an anti-federalist, at the Virginia ratifying convention); *id.* at 467 (quoting Edmund Randolph, a federalist, at the same convention).

acceptance are satisfied. Contract principles provide some guidance for all four of the situations outlined above.[189]

The first situation arises when all applications seem to address the same subject, but some are inherently inconsistent with others. For example, the thirty-three applications issued in the 1960s for a convention to partially overturn the Supreme Court's reapportionment decisions were divided between those authorizing any amendment on the subject and those authorizing *only* an amendment applying to one house of each state legislature. Similarly, many twentieth century balanced budget applications attempted to restrict the convention to verbatim text, but the text prescribed by different applications varied.[190] A 2010 Florida application (superseded by a broader one in 2014) applied for a balanced budget amendment but required that it comply with a long list of conditions not appearing in other applications.

Both contract principles and common sense dictate that applications with fundamentally inconsistent terms should not be aggregated together: According to the classical "mirror image" rule, the offer and the acceptance must match in order to form a contract.[191]

The second situation arises when some applications ask for a convention addressing Subject A while others ask for a convention addressing both Subject A and unrelated Subject B. At one time, I believed those applications could be aggregated as to Subject A, but that result is inconsistent with contract principles. In this case, as in the first situation, the applications seek quite different conventions. If the convention were to address only Subject A, then the expectations of one group of applicants would not be met; but if a convention were

---

[189] The contract analogy occurred to me in part because I did extensive work in contracts while in law practice and occasionally taught the subject as a law professor. More importantly, in writing this I have had the advantage of guidance by Scott Burnham, the Frederick N. & Barbara T. Curley Professor of Law at Gonzaga University, who is one of the nation's premier scholars on the law of contracts.

[190] Aside from aggregation issues, such applications may not be valid. *See supra* § 3.8.4.

[191] *See* RESTATEMENT (SECOND) OF CONTRACTS § 58 (1981).

empowered to address both subjects, it would fail to meet the expectations of the other group. Put another way, the "offer" is materially different from the purported "acceptance."[192]

This non-aggregation conclusion is supported by correspondence between states negotiating the 1776–1777 Providence Convention. When Massachusetts called a convention to consider paper money and public credit, Connecticut (after an initial rejection) sought to accept on the basis of paper money, public credit, and military affairs. The response from Massachusetts president James Bowdoin indicated that an additional subject would be welcome, but stopped short of committing himself until he had seen Connecticut's proposal in writing.[193]

Of course, just as an offeror is the master of his offer, a state is the master of its application. Certainly a state is free, when applying for a convention on two unrelated subjects, to specify that its application should be aggregated with others limited to either subject.

In the third situation, one set of applications contemplates a convention addressing Subject A while another set contemplates a convention addressing Subject X, which encompasses Subject A. For example, the first group may seek a balanced budget convention while the second seeks fiscal restraints on the federal government. In this case, contract principles argue for aggregation on Subject A.[194]

Admittedly, the states applying for "fiscal restraints" might have preferred alternatives other than a balanced budget amendment. However, they employed language broad enough to comprehend a balanced budget amendment, a widely known form of judicial re-

---

[192] If, however, the wording of an "A plus B" application was such that the addition of B was a mere inquiry or suggestion, then presumably it could be aggregated with those applications addressing only Subject A. *Cf.* *id.* § 39.

[193] Natelson, *Conventions*, supra note 2, at 640–42.

[194] As Professor Burnham points out: in the absence of qualifying language "if the offeror said, for example, 'I offer you any of my household furniture,' and the offeree responded, 'I'll buy the couch,' there is no doubt a contract was formed with respect to the couch."

straint. They could have defined the subject as "fiscal restraints on the federal government, *excluding* a balanced budget amendment." But they did not.

The conclusion of aggregability in the third situation is strengthened by a prudential factor: Any state that, faced with the choice between a balanced budget amendment and no restraints at all, would prefer no restraints at all, still retains multiple remedies. It may:

- Rescind or amend its application before the thirty-four state threshold is reached;
- Join at the convention with the non-applying states in voting against a balanced budget proposal; and
- Join with non-applying states in refusing to ratify.

The conclusion of aggregability is further strengthened by historical precedent: An application is a resolution of a state legislature conditionally authorizing and directing Congress call a convention on the topics listed in the application. Both before and after the Founding, states frequently have authorized their commissioners to participate in conventions with restricted subject matter by granting their commissioners power including, but wider than, that subject matter.[195]

In the fourth situation, some applications address Subject A and others petition for a plenary amendments convention. Should a plenary application count toward a convention on Subject A? It may be possible to answer that question from the wording of the application.[196] For example, in March, 1861, the Illinois legislature adopted

---

[195] Natelson, *Counting, supra* note 117, at 57–59.

[196] Professor Burnham notes:

> As a matter of interpretation, we must again determine what the offeror [i.e., an applying state legislature] intended. The offeror could be saying in effect, 'I am open to discuss any topic,' leaving the offeree to choose the topic; alternatively, the offeror could be saying in effect, 'I am open to discuss only all topics,' barring the offeree from narrowing the chosen topics.

a plenary application that appears still to be valid. Its gist was that if dissatisfaction is sufficiently widespread to induce enough other states, when counted with Illinois, to apply for a convention, then for the sake of unity Illinois will meet with them.[197] This statement evinces a willingness to convene with other states, whatever they wish to discuss.

As the date indicates, Illinois' application was a response to suggestions that the states use Article V to avoid the Civil War. But the application's language is not limited to that situation and its general principle extends well beyond any one crisis. The application seems aggregable with all others.

In the usual case, however, a plenary application merely calls for a convention without adding the "welcoming" language appearing in the 1861 Illinois resolution. An advocate for aggregation might contend that this fourth scenario is really a version of the third, and that therefore a convention should be held on Subject A. Furthermore, an advocate for aggregation might assert that when a legislature passes an application for a convention to consider any and all topics, the leg-

---

[197] The application provides in part:

WHEREAS, although the people of the State of Illinois do not desire any change in our Federal constitution, yet as several of our sister States have indicated that they deem it necessary that some amendment should be made thereto; and whereas, in and by the fifth article of the constitution of the United States, provision is made for proposing amendments to that instrument, either by congress or by a convention; and whereas a desire has been expressed, in various parts of the United States, for a convention to propose amendments to the constitution; therefore,

Be it resolved by the General Assembly of the State of Illinois, That if an application shall be made to Congress, by any of the States deeming themselves aggrieved, to call a convention, in accordance with the constitutional provision aforesaid, to propose amendments to the constitution of the United States, that the Legislature of the State of Illinois will and does hereby concur in making such application.

1861 Ill. Laws 495.

islature is chargeable with recognizing that the convention may do so. If the legislature objects to the content of other applications, it may resort to the same remedies available to a dissenting state in the third situation: rescission, amendment, action at the convention, and refusal to ratify.

An opponent of aggregation might respond that in this situation, unlike the third, there is no subject-matter nexus between the two groups of applications. Everyone understands that "fiscal restraints" may include a balanced budget amendment; indeed, at the state level a balanced budget rule is a common kind of fiscal restraint. But a legislature adopting a plenary application may have had completely different issues on its collective mind, or it may have contemplated reform only in the context of a wider constitutional examination.

In this case, it seems, there is no answer based on logic alone. However, Justice Oliver Wendell Holmes, Jr. famously observed that "a page of history is worth a volume of logic"—and fortunately, history provides guidance in this instance.

An application is a conditional authorization and direction to Congress call a convention on the topics listed in the application.[198] Although we do not have an historical instance of aggregating plenary and limited applications toward an Article V convention, we can refer to convention practice governing other documents based on the same general principles.

Specifically, convention records demonstrate that states often have authorized their commissioners to participate in limited conventions by issuing plenary credentials. Further, limited conventions have routinely seated commissioners with plenary credentials.[199] Thus, both states and conventions have assumed that a commissioner with wider authority may participate fully in a convention of narrower scope—in other words, that their powers may be aggregated. For example, Connecticut issued plenary commissions to authorize its representatives to participate in the limited-subject 1777 Springfield Convention. Several states employed plenary credentials to empower

---

[198] *Supra* § 3.8.2.

[199] For examples, see Natelson, *Counting, supra* note 117, at 57–59.

their commissioners to the limited-subject Washington Conference Convention of 1861.[200]

There also are many examples of states adopting plenary applications on the assumption that they were aggregable with more limited applications. One illustration is the 1789 plenary application of New York, which the legislature intended for Congress to aggregate with Virginia's more limited application adopted the previous year. The 1899–1912 application campaign for direct election of Senators is a source of additional illustrations.[201]

So it does appear that in this aspect of convention practice the governing rule is the legal maxim that the greater includes the lesser: When counting toward a convention on a limited subject or subjects, Congress should add plenary applications to the applications limited to those subjects. Of course, the reverse is not true: Applications explicitly limited by subject should not be counted toward a plenary convention.

§ 3.10. Selecting Commissioners

At the convention, each participating state is represented by a "committee" (delegation) of commissioners (delegates). When Article V was adopted, the nearly-universal procedure was for the state legislatures to determine the method for selecting commissioners. (Exceptions were limited to instances when the selection had to be made during the legislative recess.) This practice continued for subsequent conventions as well. Article V indirectly confirms that the method of delegate selection is a prerogative of the state legislature by granting application power to state legislatures in their capacity not as branches of state government but as free-standing assemblies.

During the Founding Era, state legislatures usually opted to select the commissioners themselves.[202] Among the fifty-five commissioners at the 1787 Constitutional Convention, for example, fifty-four

---

[200] *Id.*. at 58–59.
[201] *Id.*, at 59.
[202] *See generally* Natelson, *Conventions, supra* note 2, at 668–70.

were legislative selections. The sole exception was James McClurg of Virginia. Governor Edmund Randolph designated Dr. McClurg, a noted physician, pursuant to legislative authorization after the legislature's original choice, Patrick Henry, refused to serve.[203]

A bicameral legislature may choose to elect commissioners by a joint vote of both houses, or by seriatim votes. As the McClurg example suggests, however, the legislature may choose a different selection method. During the Founding Era, state legislatures occasionally delegated the choice to the executive or to a legislative committee. A number of states attending the 1861 Washington Conference Convention permitted the governor to nominate commissioners, subject to state senate approval, and commissioners to the 1922 Santa Fe convention all were selected by state governors pursuant to legislative authorization.

In theory, a state legislature could devolve election of commissioners upon the people, voting at large or in districts. This would be unprecedented, however, and probably unwise. The commissioner's job is primarily filled with diplomatic and drafting duties; basic policy decisions are left in the commissioning legislature. The text, history, and applicable case law strongly suggest that the commissioner is also subject to legislative rather than popular instruction. Direct election could create conflicts of interest in that respect.

§ 3.11. Empowering Commissioners

As their name indicates, commissioners are empowered by a document usually called a *commission*, although the term *credentials* is also used.[204] The commission includes the name of the commissioning authority (in this case, the state legislature or its designee), the name of the commissioner, the method of selection, the assembly to which the commissioner is being sent, and language granting power to the commissioner and defining the scope of that power. When the convention opens, commissioners are expected to present their

---

[203] 3 FARRAND'S RECORDS, *supra* note 48, at 562–63.
[204] *See generally* Natelson, *Conventions, supra* note 2, at 668–70.

credentials, usually to a credentials committee, for review. Several forms from prior conventions are included in Section 4.3 below.

§ 3.12. Instructing and Supervising Commissioners

In prior federal conventions, state officials issuing commissions often supplemented them with additional written instructions.[205] Unlike the commissions, these instructions customarily were secret in order to preserve diplomatic and negotiating leverage. The instructions defined the commissioner's authority with greater precision and informed him what measures he could or could not consider, and what goals to seek. An historical sample of instructions is included in Section 4.4 below.

§ 3.13. "No Runaway" Acts and Similar Laws

Several states have adopted, or considered, measures designed to further minimize the negligible chance that a convention for proposing amendments might exceed its authority. Such measures are not enforceable to the extent they attempt to dictate the structure of a future legislature's applications, how a future legislature selects its commissioners, or the conditions under which a future legislature may recall them.[206] These measures also are not enforceable to the extent that they attempt to control the convention's discretion within the scope of its authority.[207] Provisions imposing civil or criminal penalties on commissioners who violate legislative instructions issued immediately before or during the convention probably are valid, however. Even insofar as they are technically invalid, they may serve an educational function, and if a state legislature voluntarily operates under them, that assembly may be deemed to have accepted them.[208]

---

[205] *E.g., id.* at 615, 631, 636, 638, 658, 663, 679, & 687.
[206] *See supra* § 3.7.
[207] *See supra* § 3.7.
[208] *See* Dyer v. Blair, 390 F. Supp. 1291 (N.D. Ill. 1975) (Stevens, J.) (holding that Article V legislature impliedly adopted provisions of state constitution).

§ 3.14. Convention Rules[209]

Drafters of proposed convention rules must be careful not to create rules that are overly detailed, overly prescriptive, or otherwise unrealistic.[210] The best way to avoid those faults is to adhere closely to historical experience. The following discussion, therefore, relies heavily on what convention practice has shown actually works. The principles employed here were incorporated in rules that proved highly successful during the 2016 Williamsburg Simulated Convention of States.

§ 3.14.1. The Legal Environment

As discussed in Section 3.5, the courts rely heavily on historical practice when interpreting the words of Article V. This is true both of the Supreme Court[211] and lower courts.[212] The history relied on by the courts includes both the period up to the time the Constitution was ratified and practice subsequent to ratification.

Prominent in historical practice—both before and after the Constitution's adoption—has been the uniform and exclusive

---

[209] The author would like to thank the seasoned lawmakers and other experts who contributed insights into the convention rules process. In the treatment that follows, these people sometimes are referred to as our "advisors."

[210] For a discussion of these considerations, see ROBERT G. NATELSON, A BRIEF ASSESSMENT OF THE PROPOSED CONVENTION RULES ADOPTED BY THE ASSEMBLY OF STATE LEGISLATURES (Heartland Institute, 2016), available at https://i2i.org/wp-content/uploads/2015/01/ASL-Rules-Assessment-Final.pdf.

[211] United States v. Sprague, 282 U.S. 716 (1931); Leser v. Garnett, 258 U.S. 130 (1922); Hawke v. Smith, 253 U.S. 221 (1920); see also Hollingsworth v. Virginia, 3 U.S. (3 Dall.) 381 (1798) (following procedure in adopting first ten amendments.

[212] See supra § 3.5; see also PAUL MASON, MASON'S MANUAL OF LEGISLATIVE PROCEDURE § 39-6 (Nat'l Conference of State Legislatures, 2010 ed.) [hereinafter MASON'S MANUAL] ("The best evidence of what are the established usages and customs is the rules as last in effect.").

prerogative of Article V assemblies to adopt their own rules.[213] Shortly before he ascended to the Supreme Court, Justice John Stevens, writing for a three-judge federal panel, explicitly recognized this prerogative.[214] The prerogative further extends to the right of a convention to judge the credentials of its delegates.[215] Occasional suggestions that Congress could impose rules on an Article V convention are not well-founded, either in history or law.[216]

The prerogative of conventions to establish their own rules does not mean that each convention acts on a blank slate. Far from it. Many, if not most, multi-state conventions have borrowed their written rules from prior multi-state conventions and from legislative bodies. For example, the rules employed by the Washington Conference Convention of 1861 derived substantially from those governing the 1787 Constitutional Convention.[217] The Nashville Convention of 1850 decided that when one of its own specifically adopted rules did not apply, it would consult Thomas Jefferson's manual of procedure for the United States Senate.[218]

---

[213] *Accord* MASON'S MANUAL, *supra* note 212, §§ 2-1, 10-4, 13-7.

[214] Dyer v. Blair, 390 F. Supp. 1291, 1306 (N.D. Ill. 1975) (Stevens, J.) (referring to power of a convention or legislature operating under Article V to establish its own rules); *see also* MASON'S MANUAL, *supra* note 212 § 71-1.

[215] Opinion of the Justices, 167 A. 176 (Me. 1933) (ratification conventions pass on the elections of their own members); *accord* MASON'S MANUAL, *supra* note 212, § 560.

[216] This is an assumption made in THOMAS H. NEILE, THE ARTICLE V CONVENTION TO PROPOSE CONSTITUTIONAL AMENDMENTS: CONTEMPORARY ISSUES FOR CONGRESS 39 (Cong. Research Serv., Mar. 7, 2014) [hereinafter CRS REPORT], a paper that shows insufficient understanding of history, recent research, or applicable law. For example, it relies on only two of the more than forty reported Article V judicial decisions.

[217] WASHINGTON CONFERENCE REPORT, *supra* note 35, at 19.

[218] RESOLUTIONS, ADDRESS, AND JOURNAL OF PROCEEDINGS OF THE SOUTHERN CONVENTION 26 (Harvey M. Watterson ed., 1850). Jefferson's Manual is now a source for procedure in the U.S. House of Representatives as well. *See* THOMAS JEFFERSON, JEFFERSON'S MANUAL, H.R. DOC. NO.

Convention rules are adaptations of a branch of the Anglo-American common law referred to as *parliamentary law* or *parliamentary common law*.[219] As the name suggests, parliamentary law owes its origin to the practices of the British Parliament, but over the years it has been refined for use in this country by numerous legislative and judicial precedents.[220] Parliamentary law applies to both private and public bodies, including legislatures and conventions.[221] An example of a rule of parliamentary law is that convention decisions are rendered by a majority of those voting.[222]

Although an assembly is free to adopt its own rules, parliamentary law standards govern whenever a specifically adopted rule does not.[223] In the case of a convention, parliamentary law controls (1) before adoption of formal rules[224] and (2) after adoption of formal rules when none of them resolves an issue.[225]

111-156 (2011), *available at* http://www.gpo.gov/fdsys/pkg/HMAN-112/pdf/HMAN-112.pdf.

[219] MASON'S MANUAL, *supra* note 212, § 44-1.

[220] *Id.* §§ 35, 38.

[221] *Cf. id.* §§ 41, 47.

[222] *Id.* §§ 50-1, 51-6, 510-1, 510-4; *see also* Rhode Island v. Palmer ("National Prohibition Cases"), 253 U.S. 350 (1920); Dyer v. Blair, 390 F. Supp. 1291, 1306 (N.D. Ill. 1975) (Stevens, J.).

Alarmists sometimes demand to know in advance of a convention what the majority necessary for decision will be. A common question is, "Can the convention act by a simple majority vote, or would a two-thirds majority be required, as in Congress, for proposing an amendment?" *See* ROBERT G. NATELSON, THE ALEC ARTICLE V HANDBOOK 35-37 (Am. Legislative Exch. Council, 3d ed. 2016), *available at* http://articlevinfocenter.com/wp-content/uploads/2018/10/2016-Article-V_FINAL_WEB.pdf (reproducing text of alarmists' questions and providing answers).

This question, of course, reveals ignorance of parliamentary common law. Somewhat more surprisingly, a recent Congressional Research Service paper reveals a similar ignorance. *See* CRS REPORT, *supra* note 216, at 39 (suggesting that a convention majority of two thirds would be appropriate).

[223] MASON'S MANUAL, *supra* note 212, §§ 32-4, 37.

[224] *Id.* § 39.6.

[225] *Id.* § 37.1.

Historically, the formal rules adopted by prior multi-state conventions have been less than comprehensive, leaving most matters to be decided by parliamentary law. Fortunately, that law is readily accessible and easy to ascertain: It is collected in *Mason's Manual of Legislative Procedure*, published by the National Conference of State Legislatures. As explained below, we recommend *Mason's Manual* as a source of guidance in absence of a formal convention rule to the contrary.

§ 3.14.2. Historical Resources

Before the Constitution was ratified, colonies and states met in convention over thirty times.[226] Since ratification, at least eight additional conventions of states have met: Hartford (1814), Nashville (1850), Montgomery (1861), Washington, D.C. (1861), St. Louis (1889), Santa Fe (1922),[227] Denver (and other locations) (1946–49), and

---

[226] *See supra* § 3.1; *List of Conventions of States and Colonies in American History*, http://articlevinfocenter.com/list-conventions-states-colonies-american-history/.

[227] The Santa Fe convention, which negotiated the Colorado River Compact, gathered at different times in four different locations, convening at various times in Washington, D.C., Phoenix, and Denver. Most of the meetings, however, including the final and climatic meetings, were held in Santa Fe.

I was unable to find a single, unified, online source of the convention proceedings. I accordingly collected them and posted them at http://articlevinfocenter.com/wp-content/uploads/2018/10/Minutes-CORiver-Commn.pdf.

Other twentieth century conventions met to negotiate interstate compacts as well, although most twentieth century compacts were negotiated more informally. One such gathering negotiated the Upper Colorado River Basin Compact, *see* http://articlevinfocenter.com/last-convention-states-ever-held/. It could be argued that the four-state Delaware River Basin Advisory Committee, which negotiated the Delaware River Basin Compact in 1959–1960, should be categorized as an additional interstate convention. Because this proposition is contestable, that gathering is not included in the totals listed here. *See* Robert G. Natelson, *A Modern Quasi-Convention of States*, HTTP://ARTICLEVINFOCENTER.COM/MODERN-QUASI-CONVENTION-STATES/.

Phoenix (2017).[228] The formal rules of many of the pre-and post-constitutional gatherings are available, and the journals or proceedings enable us to reconstruct a partial list of rules from many of the others.

The records from the following meetings are particularly helpful[229]:

- Albany Congress (1754)
- Stamp Act Congress (1765)
- First Continental Congress (1774)
- First Providence Convention (1776–1777)
- York Town Convention (1777)
- Springfield Convention (1777)
- New Haven Convention (1778)
- First Hartford Convention (1779)
- Philadelphia Price Convention (1780)
- Boston Convention (1780)
- Second Hartford Convention (1780)
- Second Providence Convention (1781)
- Annapolis Convention (1786)
- The Constitutional Convention (1787)
- Third Hartford Convention (1814)

---

[228] *List of Conventions of States and Colonies in American History*, http://articlevinfocenter.com/list-conventions-states-colonies-american-history/.

[229] Summaries of all but the last seven can be found in Natelson, *Conventions, supra* note 2.

The text above lists these meetings under their usual or (where available) official names. Many had other names, including informal ones. For example, the Boston Convention sometimes was referred to as the "Boston Committee"; and although the first three are now remembered as "congresses," people also applied the word "convention" to them. The term "congress" to describe a multi-state convention fell into disuse after establishment of a permanent U.S. legislature called "Congress."

- Nashville Convention (1850) (also called the Southern Convention)
- Montgomery Convention (1861)
- Washington Conference Convention (1861) (also informally called the Washington Peace Conference)
- Santa Fe Convention (1922) (formally the Colorado River Commission)[230]
- Upper Colorado River Basin Commission (1946–49)
- Phoenix Balanced Budget Amendment Planning Convention (2017)

The rules and protocols followed by these gatherings show far more commonalties than differences. For several reasons, however, the rules and protocols of the Washington Conference Convention of 1861 seem particularly apt. It was our second-most recent general multi-state convention,[231] and more states were formally represented there than at any other. It was called for the purpose of proposing amendments. So even though it did not operate under Article V, it served as prototype for a duly called convention for proposing amendments. Furthermore, the Washington rules were based heavily on those of earlier conventions. In several places below, therefore, this section focuses on the rules of the Washington conclave.[232] It also relies somewhat on the recommended rules issued by the Phoenix Balanced Budget Amendment Planning Convention,[233] rules

---

[230] Although called a "commission," this gathering was a true regional convention of states. It should not be confused with those bodies called "commissions" that operate *after and pursuant to* compacts. The latter represent another form of multi-state cooperation, but their permanent character disqualifies them from being called conventions.

[231] A "general convention" is one to which all states, or at least states from all regions, are invited, irrespective of whether all participate. It is to be distinguished from a regional, or partial, convention. *See supra* § 3.1. The term "general convention" does *not* designate an assembly where the subject matter is unlimited, as some have assumed.

[232] *Infra* § 3.14.4–.5.

[233] These rules are available at JOURNAL, *supra* note 11.

which, although still untried and perhaps overly long, represent a well-thought-out modern draft by experienced legislators.

§ 3.14.3. Formalities before Adoption of Rules

Time and Place

The congressional call specifies the initial time and place of meeting.[234] State applications cannot control the initial time and place, although state legislatures may make recommendations on those subjects to Congress. After convening, the assembly assumes control of times and places of meeting. Thus, the convention decides when and for how long to adjourn, and to what place. For example, the Nashville Convention held its initial session in June of 1850, and then adjourned to November of the same year. Twentieth century conventions negotiating Western water compacts had to address complicated engineering, geologic, and other scientific issues, so they adjourned temporarily and reconvened in different places. The Colorado River Commission (Santa Fe Convention) met in Washington, D.C., Phoenix, Denver, and Santa Fe. But Santa Fe was the site of the last eighteen of the twenty-seven meetings and of the most important negotiations.[235] The Upper Colorado River Basin Compact Commission met intermittently from July, 1946 to August, 1949. It held formal meetings in five cities and towns and held public hearings in four more.[236]

---

[234] *See supra* § 3.9.

[235] For a unified, online collection of the proceedings, see MINUTES AND RECORDS OF THE COLORADO RIVER COMMISSION (1922) [hereinafter COLORADO COMMISSION RECORDS], *available at* http://articlevinfocenter.com/wp-content/uploads/2018/10/Minutes-CORiver-Commn.pdf.

[236] Article V Information Center, *The Last Convention of States Held Before Phoenix in 2017: The Upper Colorado River Commission,* http://articlevinfocenter.com/last-convention-states-ever-held/.

Commissioner Selection

A multi-state convention is a gathering of states or state legislatures and their participants may choose their own representatives. Accordingly, selection of state committees is *always* left to the states sending them.[237] The strength of the rule is illustrated by the outcomes of the rare attempts to breach it: Only twice has the calling entity attempted to guide the selection procedure (in 1765 and again in 1780), and on both occasions those efforts were successfully disregarded.[238] In any event, for Congress to dictate how commissioners are selected would radically undercut the fundamental purpose of the convention procedure as a way for the states to bypass Congress.

The selection method most often chosen by state legislatures has been election by the legislature itself, either in joint session or (more often) seriatim by chamber. However, legislatures may delegate the choice to the executive alone or to some combination of executive nomination and legislative approval. The latter methods were employed for many of the commissioners sent to Washington (1861) and to all of them sent to Santa Fe (1922).

Commissioner Credentialing

Each state determines how to commission its own representatives. Early in the convention, each commissioner is expected to present his or her *credentials*—that is, the commission or comparable

---

[237] *See supra* § 3.10.

[238] When the Massachusetts legislature called the 1765 Stamp Act Congress, it asked that other colonies select commissioners through only the lower houses of their legislatures. This was because at the time only the lower chambers were directly elected, while the upper chambers were controlled indirectly by the British Crown. Nevertheless, several colonies chose commissioners in ways other than that recommended, and those commissioners were duly seated. Natelson, *Conventions, supra* note 2, at 635–37. In 1780, the Massachusetts legislature called a convention of five northeastern states. Apparently because some state legislatures were in recess, it asked that commissioners be appointed by those states' official "councils of war." Several states opted to select commissioners by other means, and they also were duly seated. *Id.* at 659–60.

document showing authority to act on behalf of his state or state legislature. The convention selects a committee that passes on those credentials.

Initial Voting Rules

As noted above, a convention for proposing amendments is a *convention of states*: a gathering of states in their sovereign, or semi-sovereign, capacities.[239] To the extent the extant records address the issue, they show that conventions of states universally apply the suffrage rule of equality among states. This rule follows from the international law standard that all sovereigns are equal. *The calling entity (which, in the case of an amendments convention, is Congress), may not alter this rule.*[240]

Although at some conventions individual commissioners have been tagged as "members," multi-state conventions never have applied a "one person, one vote" rule. Perhaps this is because, technically, the "members" of the convention are not individual commissioners but state committees.[241]

Some multi-state convention journals refer to voting "by ballot," especially for officers and committees. This phrase does not refer to voting per capita, but to a procedure by which individual choices are secret, even within state committees.[242] State committees still vote as

---

[239] *Supra* § 3.2.4.

[240] In 1783 the Massachusetts legislature attempted to break this custom by calling a five-state "one delegate, one vote" convention. The call had to be rescinded when two of the four other states invited refused to attend. Natelson, *Conventions, supra* note 2, at 666.

[241] *Cf.* MASON'S MANUAL, *supra* note 212, § 52 (providing for equality of the "members" of an assembly).

[242] 1 FARRAND'S RECORDS, *supra* note 48, at 2 ("The Members then proceeded to ballot on behalf of their respective States—and, the ballots being taken, it appeared that the said George Washington was unanimously elected."); *see also id.* at 4: ("Mr. Wilson moved that a Secretary be appointed, and nominated Mr. Temple Franklin. Col. Hamilton nominated Major Jackson. On the ballot Majr. Jackson had 5 votes & Mr. Franklin 2 votes."); *id.* at 29 (showing only eight slash marks representing votes). Obviously, since

units. However, most voting is not by ballot but *viva voce* (Latin for "with live voice").[243]

The tradition at general conventions has been for state-by-state votes to be tabulated in northeast-to-southwest order. Because of the current configuration of the country another method—such as alphabetical order—may be more appropriate today.

Quorum and Majority Vote

There are two kinds of quorum rules: (1) the number of commissioners who must agree to cast a state committee's vote and (2) the number of states necessary to transact business on the floor. The former is called an *internal quorum rule*. It is determined by the commissioning authority—that is, by each state for its own committee. For example, when New York commissioned its three delegates to the Constitutional Convention, it specified that any two must be present (and agree) to cast the state's vote.

As for the quorum of states necessary on the floor and the margin required for decision, by both common law and court decision a majority of states participating in the gathering is necessary for a quorum,[244] and a majority of states voting (a quorum being present) is necessary to decide.[245]

---

there were several dozen commissioners present, this low vote tally had to reflect the states.

[243] MASON'S MANUAL, *supra* note 212, §§ 306-2, 536.

[244] *Id.* §§ 49-1, 502-1; *see also id.* § 501-1 ("The total membership of a body is to be taken as the basis for computing a quorum, but when there is a vacancy, unless a special provision is applicable, a quorum will consist of the majority of the members remaining qualified."); accord *id.* § 502-2.

Section 501-2 provides that "The authority that creates a body has the power to fix its quorum." In the case of an amendments convention, however, that authority is the convention—not Congress, which calls it, nor the state legislatures, who apply for it and authorize and create its delegations. The Constitution does not prescribe a quorum, leaving it to the convention.

[245] Rhode Island v. Palmer ("National Prohibition Cases"), 253 U.S. 350 (1920); Dyer v. Blair, 390 F. Supp. 1291, 1306 (N.D. Ill. 1975) (Stevens,

What Officers Should the Convention Have?

Conventions of states always decide what officers are to govern them. Prior conventions seem to have made this decision pursuant to parliamentary law, before formal rules were adopted.

At the least, every convention has a presiding officer, called the president or chairman, and a secretary, executive secretary, or clerk.[246] Some conventions, especially larger ones, have selected other officers, such as vice president, assistant secretaries, doorkeepers, sergeants-at-arms, and messengers. One former legislator consulted on this project recommended appointment of a parliamentarian. This recommendation was accepted by the 2016 Williamsburg Simulated Convention and by the 2017 Phoenix Planning Convention. The latter conclave also recommended that the vice president be designated as convention manager, "with the duties to provide necessary facilities, staff, audio visual equipment, and document reproduction at the direction of the Convention and the committees."[247]

How Officers Are Chosen.

In prior conventions, the identity of the temporary presiding officer, pending election of a permanent president, seems to have been arranged in informal pre-opening meetings. Although some have suggested that Congress designate a temporary presiding officer in its convention call, no multi-state convention call has ever done this, and an attempt to do so would have advisory force only.

At the 1754 Albany Congress, a representative of the Crown was present and became the presiding officer. Since Independence, permanent officers invariably have been elected by the convention itself, generally before adoption of formal rules, pursuant to parliamentary law. To the extent the historical records are complete, they show that

---

J.). On majorities as a rule of decision, see MASON'S MANUAL, *supra* note 212, §§ 50-1, 51-6, 510-1, 510-4.

[246] MASON'S MANUAL, *supra* note 212, § 584 refers to the secretary, executive secretary or clerk in a legislature as the "chief legislative officer."

[247] Convention Resolution 1, Recommended Rules, § 2.1.2.2.2, in JOURNAL, *supra* note 11 (unpaginated, but on sheet 273).

all American multi-government conventions have elected officers by a majority vote of state committees. This was true even at the 1922 Colorado River Commission, where a federal representative, Secretary of Commerce Herbert Hoover, was present. Hoover ultimately did serve as chairman, but only after free election by his fellow commissioners, one from each participating state.[248]

Before the 1850 Nashville Convention, a preliminary committee decided on nominees for various offices. Although this did not prevent nominations from the floor, the convention did elect the committee's nominees.

The presiding officer always has been elected from among the commissioners rather than from outside the convention. The secretary or clerk usually (but not always) has been a non-commissioner, presumably to better assure impartiality in preparation and preservation of the records. We recommend that state lawmakers consult in advance on preliminary nominations, and that a convention of states retain the custom of electing a commissioner as the presiding officer and a non-commissioner as secretary or clerk. Although most conventions have elected the secretary or clerk, the Phoenix Planning Convention recommended that that officer, together with the sergeant-at-arms and parliamentarian, be appointed by the president.

How Rules Are Adopted.

Some of the smaller conventions have included only a handful of commissioners—most of them veterans of government service or prior conventions—thereby obviating the need to adopt formal rules. The 1778 New Haven Convention adopted rules, but did not insert them in the journal. The 1922 Santa Fe Convention (Colorado River Commission) seems not to have adopted formal rules, but it did vote on agendas and procedures for each future meeting.[249] In the absence of formal rules, parliamentary law, essentially as represented by *Ma-*

---

[248] Because of Hoover's relief work in World War I and his reputation as an international engineer, his personal prestige at the time was enormous.

[249] For a unified, online source of this convention's proceedings, see COLORADO COMMISSION RECORDS, *supra* note 235.

son's Manual, prevails.²⁵⁰ The larger conventions all adopted formal rules and entered them on the journal, although parliamentary law served as a source of default rules.²⁵¹

During preparation of this treatise, an experienced state lawmaker suggested that an informal committee of state legislative leaders draft proposed rules in advance of the convention, and then try to induce as many state legislatures as possible to agree to them in advance. In a similar vein, the 2017 Phoenix Planning Convention recommended rules for a future convention for proposing a balanced budget amendment. Whether or not such preliminary work is performed, the final decision on convention rules belongs to the convention itself.

Immediately after election of officers, the convention should choose a rules committee. By modern parliamentary law, committee staffing is the prerogative of the presiding officer.²⁵² However, the convention may vote to select the committee itself,²⁵³ and the historical records suggest that most major conventions have done so. In absence of a rule to the contrary, whoever staffs the committee designates the person who chairs it.²⁵⁴

After drafting proposed rules, the committee presents those rules to the floor for debate, adoption, or rejection.

§ 3.14.4. Recommended Rules Not Pertaining to Debate or Decorum

Source of Default Rules

A "default rule" is a rule that applies in absence of an explicit rule to the contrary. For example, in Anglo-American parliamentary practice, the default rule for making decisions is a majority of those

---

[250] MASON'S MANUAL, *supra* note 212, §§ 32-4, 37.
[251] Default rules are discussed below in Section 3.14.4.
[252] MASON'S MANUAL, *supra* note 212, § 600-1.
[253] *Id.* § 600-2.
[254] *Id.* § 608.

voting.[255] The federal Constitution, or that of a state, or the adopted rules of a public body, can alter a default rule.

It is impractical for a temporary gathering such as a convention of states to adopt rules to address every conceivable situation, and the historical record shows that conventions of states have not attempted to do so. Instead, like legislatures, they have adopted discrete rules addressed to particular situations and relied on a common source to supply the gaps.[256] By way of illustration, the default rules for the 1787 Constitutional Convention appear to have been adapted from the procedures of the Confederation Congress. The 1850 Nashville Convention formally acceded to Thomas Jefferson's *Manual of Parliamentary Practice,* which Jefferson drafted for the U.S. Senate when he served as Vice President, and therefore as President of the Senate.

The best modern option for a source of default rules is *Mason's Manual of Legislative Procedure.* There are several reasons for this.

First, *Mason's Manual* is very comprehensive. Using it as a source of default rules would make it unnecessary for the convention to struggle with such questions as which motions are in order and when, or the vote margin required for reconsideration.

Second, *Mason's Manual* is usable and practical. Not only is it time-tested, but unlike the rules and prior default sources used by earlier conventions, it has been kept up-to-date and consistent with modern technology.

Third, *Mason's Manual* relies on parliamentary common law, and is annotated heavily with legislative and judicial precedents, so the sources and reasoning behind a particular rule are easily discoverable.

---

[255] This rule was established in the famous case of *Oldknow v. Wainright,* [K.B. 1760] 2 Burr. 1017, 97 Eng. Rep. 683 (Mansfield, C.J.).

[256] MASON'S MANUAL, *supra* note 212, § 30-1 ("Most legislative bodies adopt a manual of legislative procedure as the authority to apply in all cases not covered by constitutional provisions, legislative rules, or statutes."); *see also id.* § 30-2 (stating that resort to manuals by "deliberative assemblies" is permissible).

Fourth, it enjoys wide currency among state legislatures: Seventy of the ninety-nine American state legislative chambers[257] have adopted it, and there is trend in its direction.[258] Therefore, *Mason's Manual*, or adopted rules based on *Mason's Manual*, are likely to be familiar to a majority of commissioners—most of whom will be chosen by state legislatures and will have had state legislative experience. *Mason's Manual* also will be familiar to any legislative officers or committees assigned to oversee their respective convention delegations.

Among those lawmakers consulted for this treatise, none was hostile to *Mason's Manual,* and several were very enthusiastic. The 2017 Phoenix Planning Convention recommended it as the source of default rules for a future amendments convention.[259]

To be sure, *Mason's Manual* was written for state legislatures rather than for conventions. As a practical matter, however, the principal implication of this fact is that certain portions of the manual, such as the portion addressing "Relations with the Executive" can be safely disregarded.[260]

Adoption of *Mason's Manual* would make it unnecessary to craft rules for every occasion. Nevertheless, some explicit rules are called for, as explained below.

Voting by State

All multi-state conventions whose journals disclose a voting rule have weighted states equally. All but one proceeded on the basis of "one state, one vote." The exception was the St. Louis convention of

---

[257] *See Using Mason's Manual of Legislative Procedure*, NAT'L CONFERENCE OF STATE LEGISLATURES, http://www.ncsl.org/research/about-state-legislatures/masons-manual-for-legislative-bodies.aspx (last visited Nov. 5, 2018).

[258] *Id.*

[259] Recommended Rule § 5.2, in JOURNAL, *supra* note 11 (unpaginated, but at sheet 278).

[260] The two most prominent rivals to *Mason's Manual* also were designed for bodies other than conventions: *Robert's Rules of Order*, and *Jefferson's Manual.*

1889, which adopted the rule of "one state, eight votes." Thus, equality of state voting power has been both the default rule and the standard prevailing when conventions adopt explicit standards of suffrage.[261]

To understand the reasons for state-by-state voting, it is important to remember that a convention for proposing amendments is not a general legislature. Nor is it an instrumentality of any one government. It is, rather, part of a process designed *explicitly* to enable the semi-sovereign states, acting as a group through their legislatures,[262] to offer ratifiable proposals. James Madison pointed out that the Constitution has both "national" (popular) and "federal" (state-based) features.[263] The amendments convention, like the U.S. Senate, is a clear example of the latter.

Moreover, the fundamental reason for the convention procedure was to provide the states a way to bypass Congress.[264] The only entity, other than the convention, that might prescribe an unprecedented voting rule would be Congress.[265] But allowing Congress to design the convention's voting system would undercut the convention's fundamental purpose in a way that the judiciary generally does not sanction. Further, there is no evidence that the one state, one vote rule has been impacted in any way by the "one person, one vote" requirement the modern Supreme Court imposes on legislative bodies with general governmental powers and directly representing the people. A convention for proposing amendments is not a legislature, does not have general governmental powers, and serves only as a "federal" (state-based) method for proposing amendments.

---

[261] For example, the rules of the 1861 Washington Conference Convention provided, "Mode of Voting. All votes shall be taken by States, and each State to give one vote. The yeas and nays of the members shall not be given or published—only the decision by States." WASHINGTON CONFERENCE REPORT, *supra* note 35, at 25.

[262] *See supra* § 3.2.4.

[263] THE FEDERALIST No. 39 (James Madison).

[264] *See supra* § 3.3.

[265] Some have argued that Congress has this power under the Necessary and Proper Clause, but this is inaccurate. *See supra* § 3.9.4.

Although the application and convention process was not intended to be perfectly democratic, it does accommodate the need for popular consent. The requirement that two thirds of states, rather than a simple majority, apply for a convention raises the probability of popular consent. The three-quarters ratification requirement virtually assures that any amendment will be approved by a majority (and more likely a supermajority) of the American people.[266]

There have been occasional attempts in multi-state conventions to challenge or alter the rule of state voting equality, invariably without success. For example, a motion to alter state voting power to reflect population differences was considered at the Nashville Convention. It was recognized that this motion would require assent by a majority of states. The motion was defeated when a majority of states refused to adopt it.[267]

Majority Voting

Approval of motions and proposals by a majority of those voting (in this case, a majority of states) is the prevailing rule under parliamentary law and prior convention practice. The convention may, if a majority of state committees wishes, alter the rule. The Santa Fe Convention (Colorado River Commission) decided on a unanimity requirement among states for most purposes.[268] The reason, apparently, was that the group was negotiating an interstate compact, the

---

[266] ROBERT G. NATELSON, PROPOSING CONSTITUTIONAL AMENDMENTS BY A CONVENTION OF THE STATES: A HANDBOOK FOR STATE LAWMAKERS 22 (Am. Legislative Exch. Council, 3d ed. 2014), *available at* https://www.alec.org/app/uploads/2016/06/2016-Article-V_FINAL_WEB.pdf.

[267] RESOLUTIONS, ADDRESS, AND JOURNAL OF PROCEEDINGS OF THE SOUTHERN CONVENTION 27 (Harvey M. Watterson ed., 1850). Similarly an effort in 1783 by the Massachusetts legislature to call a one delegate, one vote convention failed because states refused to participate. Natelson, *Conventions, supra* note 2, at 666.

[268] COLORADO COMMISSION RECORDS, *supra* note 235

compact would not be binding on any state that rejected it, and the compact might be useless unless all states consented.

The unanimity requirement at the Santa Fe meetings worked tolerably well, but there were only eight commissioners (one from each state and a federal representative, Secretary of Commerce Herbert Hoover), and dissenters occasionally voted "yes" so as not to obstruct the progress of the negotiations. Even at Santa Fe, late in the proceedings the unanimity rule was changed temporarily to majority consent for most purposes.[269]

A unanimous voting rule clearly would not be appropriate at a general convention, with far more states involved. Moreover, requiring a supermajority of states to propose, as some have suggested, would upset the carefully balanced structure of Article V and impair its purpose of giving the states equal proposing power with Congress.[270] Amendments conventions, therefore, should decide substantive and procedural questions by a majority of states voting, a quorum being present. In recommending rules to a future amendments convention, the 2017 Phoenix Planning Convention adopted this view.[271]

Quorum

Traditionally, a quorum is a majority of eligible voters (states),[272] and this rule seems to have been followed for most multi-

---

[269] *Id.*

[270] ROBERT G. NATELSON, A BRIEF ASSESSMENT OF THE PROPOSED CONVENTION RULES ADOPTED BY THE ASSEMBLY OF STATE LEGISLATURES 7 (Heartland Institute, 2016), *available at* https://i2i.org/wp-content/uploads/2015/01/ASL-Rules-Assessment-Final.pdf (pointing out how Article V's requirements for Congress and for the convention offset each other: Congress needs only a majority to consider, but a supermajority to propose; the states need a super-majority to begin collective consideration, but only a majority to propose. Requiring state proposals to attain *two* super-majorities would put them at a disadvantage compared to Congress, contrary to the goal of Article V).

[271] Sections 3.2.2 & 3.2.3.

[272] MASON'S MANUAL, *supra* note 212, § 500-2.

state conventions. For example, the 1787 Constitutional Convention adopted a quorum of seven—that is, a majority of state committees—with decisions to be made by a majority of a quorum. On the other hand, the Washington Conference Convention adopted a quorum of only seven states when twenty-one were present.[273] In absence of unforeseen circumstances, there is no reason to depart from the majority rule, and the proposed rules of the Phoenix Planning Convention adopted this view.[274] However, any future convention of states should provide, as prior multi-state conventions have, that if a quorum is not present, those states that are represented should have power to adjourn from day to day.

Prayers and Oaths

Some conventions have been introduced with prayers, generally before the daily session. For example, the rules of the Hartford Convention of 1814 prescribed that "[t]he meetings of this Convention shall be opened each morning, by prayer, which it is requested may be performed, alternately, by the Chaplains of the Legislature of Connecticut, residing in the city of Hartford."[275] Even the modern Congress has decided that prayer can have an uplifting effect on the proceedings.

On the other hand, the most successful American multi-state convention in history—the one that drafted the Constitution—made no provision for institutionalized prayer.

The Albany Congress of 1754 administered an oath to its secretary, presumably to record the proceedings honestly. Oaths of fidelity are routinely administered to American public officers, and there seems to be no reason why a convention should not do so as well.

---

[273] WASHINGTON CONFERENCE REPORT, *supra* note 35, at 23.

[274] JOURNAL, *supra* note 11.

[275] A SHORT ACCOUNT OF THE HARTFORD CONVENTION 24 (Theodore Lyman ed., 1823).

Kinds of Committees

A convention may decide to create any committees relevant to its mission. Typically, conventions create committees to review credentials, draft language, and negotiate differences. If the gathering is called under applications that mention several subjects, the convention may opt to create a committee to develop amendment language addressing each subject.

Committee Staffing

Under modern parliamentary common law, the presiding officer staffs committees, as did the president of the 1814 Hartford Convention. An assembly may, however, provide for election instead. A rule of the 1787 Constitutional Convention specified:

> That Committees shall be appointed by ballot; and that the members who have the greatest number of ballots, although not a majority of the votes present, be the Committee. When two or more Members have an equal number of votes, the Member standing first on the list in the order of taking down the ballots shall be preferred.[276]

Note that under this rule election was by a plurality rather than a majority and that "ballot" meant secret ballot.

There seems to be no reason to go through the trouble of electing members to all committees, but election may be appropriate for major areas of responsibility, such as rules and intra-convention negotiation.

Secrecy

Pre-twentieth century conventions appear to have applied a rule of secrecy. A principal purpose was to allow commissioners to think aloud, debate freely, and change their minds without losing face. For example, the rules of the First Continental Congress provided that "the doors be kept shut during the time of business, and that the members consider themselves under the strongest obligations of honour, to keep the proceedings secret, untill [sic] the majority shall di-

---

[276] 1 FARRAND'S RECORDS, *supra* note 48, at 9.

rect them to be made public."[277] The 1861 Washington Conference Convention prescribed that "[t]he yeas and nays of the members shall not be given or published—only the decision by States."[278]

Similarly, the rules of both the Constitutional and Washington Conference Conventions specified that "no copy be taken of any entry on the journal during the sitting of the House without leave of the House," and that "members only be permitted to inspect the journal."[279] The Constitutional Convention rules admonished that "nothing spoken in the House be printed, or otherwise published or communicated without leave."[280]

The 1946–49 Upper Colorado Basin Compact Commission seems to have opened much of its work to the public, and advisors consulted during the preparation of this treatise were unanimous in affirming that such secrecy would not be publicly acceptable today. *Mason's Manual*, accordingly, includes no such rules. Advocates of secrecy may be comforted by the realization that, although secrecy has some procedural advantages, disclosure offers some offsetting advantages (in addition to public acceptance). Among these advantages is the greater ability of legislative authorities to ensure that their commissioners remain within their instructions and remain connected with political realities.

Obviously, openness does not justify chaos: The convention will have to adopt rules assuring that its proceedings are not disrupted by outsiders. But this is no more than any modern legislative body must do.[281]

---

[277] 1 JOURNALS OF THE CONTINENTAL CONGRESS 1774–1789, at 26 (Worthington Chauncey Ford et al. eds., 1904).

[278] WASHINGTON CONFERENCE REPORT, *supra* note 35, at 25.

[279] 1 FARRAND'S RECORDS, *supra* note 48, at 15; WASHINGTON CONFERENCE REPORT, *supra* note 35, at 25.

[280] 1 FARRAND'S RECORDS, *supra* note 48, at 15.

[281] MASON'S MANUAL, *supra* note 212, § 705-3 (providing that a legislative body has absolute control of its chambers).

Minutes

All conventions direct the secretary, either personally or through a convention-authorized assistant, to record the minutes necessary for entry in the official journal. A 1787 Constitutional Convention rule specified that "Immediately after the President shall have taken the Chair, and the members their seats, the minutes of the preceding day shall be read by the Secretary."[282]

Number of Commissioners on the Floor

Informal discussions among state legislative leaders prior to a convention may result in agreed limits on the size of any one state's committee. A study of the historical record suggests that a cap of five commissioners per state would be appropriate. Ultimately, however, the size of a state's committee is for that state's legislature to determine.

It is possible that non-cooperative states may, if they do not boycott the convention,[283] opt to send oversized delegations. They may do so as a measure of protest, as a populist gesture, or as a way of skewing debate in their favor. By way of illustration Tennessee sent a hundred commissioners to the Nashville Convention, although all the remaining states collectively sent only seventy-five. The presence of oversized committees does not change the one state, one vote rule (which, in fact, survived a challenge at Nashville), but such a situation could present problems of crowding and fairness.

One way to respond is to adopt a convention rule limiting the number of commissioners from any one state who may participate in any given debate or appear on the floor at one time. Another response is a limit on the amount of floor time used on any day by any state committee.

---

[282] 1 FARRAND'S RECORDS, *supra* note 48, at 8.

[283] For example, Rhode Island objected to the 1787 Constitutional Convention, and refused to send commissioners. No multi-state convention has included committees from every single state.

Costs

Traditionally, each state sending commissioners to a convention of the states bore the cost of its own delegation. Common facilities, particularly a hall, were donated, either by the host state or by private parties.

Today, however, common facilities are likely to consist of more than a hall: They will include technology and supplies as well. Moreover, to modern eyes donations by private parties may seem suspect. The Phoenix Planning Convention's recommended rules resolved the issue of cost by affirming that each state was required to maintain its own delegation, and that common costs were to be divided among all states equally.[284]

§ 3.14.5. Rules of Debate and Decorum

Several of the major multi-state conventions have adopted rules of debate and decorum specific to their needs. Notable among these are the standards applied at the Washington Conference Convention of 1861, which were based largely, although not entirely, on the rules of debate and decorum in the more famous conclave in Philadelphia in 1787.[285] For reasons mentioned earlier, the Washington Convention rules are worth examining in some detail.[286] Listed below are the principal Washington Convention rules together with commentary that may be helpful in adapting them to modern needs.[287]

Order of Business

The Washington Convention rules prescribed that (1) "[i]mmediately after the President shall have taken the chair, and the members their seats, the minutes of the preceding day shall be read by the Secretary" and that (2) "[o]rders of the day shall be read next

---

[284] Recommended Rule § 6.1, in JOURNAL, *supra* note 11 (unpaginated, but at sheet 279)

[285] WASHINGTON CONFERENCE REPORT, *supra* note 35, at 19.

[286] *Supra* § 3.14.2.

[287] All the rules of that convention are not treated here—only those on debate and decorum.

after the minutes, and either discussed or postponed, before any other business shall be introduced."[288]

Mason's Manual sets forth a somewhat different order.[289] If one disregards the items on *Mason's* list relevant to a legislature but not to a convention, one is left with the following: (1) call to order, (2) roll call, (3) invocation, (4) reading and approval of the journal of the previous day, (5) reports of standing committees, (6) reports of special or select committees, (7) special orders, (8) unfinished business, (9) introduction and first reading of proposals, (10) consideration of daily calendar, (11) announcement of committee meetings, and (12) adjournment.

Focus of the Convention

Another rule of the Washington Convention provided as follows: "Every member, rising to speak, shall address the President; and while he shall be speaking none shall pass between them, or hold discourse with another, or read a book, pamphlet, or paper, printed or manuscript; and of two members rising to speak at the same time, the President shall name him who shall first be heard."[290]

Addressing the presiding officer is in accord with modern practice.[291] The presiding officer's obligation to select the person rising earlier, and to choose between those rising at the same time, also is consistent.[292] The proscription on reading extraneous matter may seem alien in a time of universal multi-tasking, particularly with tablet computers and smartphones; but there is something to be said for requiring commissioners to direct their attention to the debate. If, however, written motions are to be disseminated instantly, commissioners should have receiving devices available. If computers are used for that purpose, then preventing commissioners from reading unrelated matter on them may be impractical.

---

[288] WASHINGTON CONFERENCE REPORT, *supra* note 35, at 23, 24.

[289] MASON'S MANUAL, *supra* note 212, § 710.

[290] WASHINGTON CONFERENCE REPORT, *supra* note 35, at 23.

[291] MASON'S MANUAL, *supra* note 212, §§ 91-2, 110-1.

[292] *Id.* § 91-3(a), (b).

Frequency and Length of Speaking

The rules of the Washington Convention further stated, "A member shall not speak oftener than twice, without special leave upon the same question; and not a second time before every other who had been silent shall have been heard, if he choose to speak upon the subject."[293]

This "two-times" rule had been used in the First Continental Congress of 1774 and in other fora, and its success argues for emulation. *Mason's Manual* provides that a person may speak only once on a question at the same stage of procedure on a given day, and sometimes even on different days.[294]

Previous to 2017, there was no multi-state convention that limited the amount of time a commissioner could speak on the floor. An effort to impose time limits at the Washington Conference Convention was unsuccessful. The rules under which the 2017 Arizona Planning Convention met provided that no state delegation could speak for more than ten minutes at a time—but the rules that assembly recommended for a future amendments convention made no reference to time limits.

Because a modern convention for proposing amendments represents more states than any prior multi-state gathering—and therefore probably would contain more commissioners—a convention should consider implementing time limits.

Motions

The Washington Convention rules specified as follows: "A motion made and seconded, shall be repeated; and if written, as it shall be when any member shall so require, read aloud by the Secretary before it shall be debated; and may be withdrawn at any time before the vote upon it shall have been declared."[295] The rules further stated that "[w]hen a debate shall arise upon a question, no

---

[293] WASHINGTON CONFERENCE REPORT, *supra* note 35, at 23–24.
[294] MASON'S MANUAL, *supra* note 212, § 102.
[295] WASHINGTON CONFERENCE REPORT, *supra* note 35, at 24.

motion, other than to amend the question, to commit it, or to postpone the debate, shall be received."[296]

Today's technology makes it more practical to require that all but the simplest, most standardized motions be written; and they can be disseminated instantly by electronic means.[297] *Mason's Manual* does not require seconds; thus in the absence of a seconder, the movant alone may withdraw.[298] As for the precedence of motions, the treatment in *Mason's Manual* should suffice.[299]

Simplifying Complex Questions

The applicable Washington rule was as follows: "A question which is complicated, shall, at the request of any member, be divided and put separately upon the propositions of which it is compounded."[300]

This rule is probably best retained, as it is more appropriate for a convention than the single-subject-related tests for bills set forth in *Mason's Manual*.[301] To avoid confusion, the term "member" should be replaced by "commissioner."

Calls to Order

The Washington rules stated that "[a] member may be called to order by another member, as well as by the President, and may be allowed to explain his conduct or expressions supposed to be reprehensible. ~~And all questions of order shall be decided by the President, without appeal or debate.~~"[302]

---

[296] *Id.*

[297] *Cf.* MASON'S MANUAL, *supra* note 212, § 144-2 ("A motion is usually presented orally, but if particularly long or involved, the presiding officer may require that it be presented . . . in writing.").

[298] *Id.* §§ 62, 157-1.

[299] *Id.* § 441 ("Form of Presenting Main Motions"); *id.* § 442 ("Precedence of Main Motions").

[300] WASHINGTON CONFERENCE REPORT, *supra* note 35, at 24.

[301] MASON'S MANUAL, *supra* note 212, §§ 311-2, 313-1, 313-2.

[302] WASHINGTON CONFERENCE REPORT, *supra* note 35, at 24.

Not even the great prestige of former President John Tyler, the Washington Convention's presiding officer, enabled the stricken non-appealability language to survive a motion to amend. The convention decided that any ruling from the chair could be appealed, although without debate.[303] This is particularly important because any person with sufficient reputation to be elected presiding officer is likely to have, or to have had, ties (and perhaps sympathies) with the same federal government the convention has gathered to reform.

The word "member" in this rule should be changed to "commissioner." *Mason's Manual* does not refer to a participant being called to order by any other participant, although the presiding officer may call anyone to order.[304]

Motions to Adjourn

The Washington Convention also adopted the following rule: "Upon a question to adjourn for the day, which may be made at any time, if it be seconded, the question shall be put without debate."[305]

In *Mason's Manual*, adjournment for the day is called a "recess," and a motion to recess is not debatable.[306] A permanent adjournment is called an adjournment *sine die* (Latin for "without day," meaning "without a day for reconvening"). A convention may adjourn *sine die* at any time, whether or not its work is complete.[307]

---

[303] *Cf.* MASON'S MANUAL, *supra* note 212, §§ 230-1, 246-4 (permitting appeals).

[304] *Id.* § 122.

[305] WASHINGTON CONFERENCE REPORT, *supra* note 35, at 24.

[306] MASON'S MANUAL, *supra* note 212, §§ 215, 216-3.

[307] *Id.* § 204-1. The Founding Generation specifically recognized that a convention for proposing amendments may adjourn without proposing any amendments. Natelson, *Rules, supra* note 21, at 743–44 n.342 (quoting James Madison and an anti-federalist writer).

Decorum on Adjournments for the Day

The Washington Convention rules provided that "When the Convention shall adjourn, every member shall stand in his place until the President pass him."[308]

This rule derived from the 1787 convention, and was a tribute to the enormous prestige of its president, General Washington. The Washington convention retained the rule, probably as a tribute to John Tyler. Whether a modern convention adopts it may depend on the personal prestige of its presiding officer.

Absences

On this topic, the Washington Convention rules stated "That no member be absent from the Convention, so as to interrupt the representation of the State, without leave."[309] This is in accord with the modern practice of compelling attendance at the "call of the house."[310]

Sitting of Committees and Assuring Proper Notice of Proposals

The Washington Convention prescribed that "Committees do not sit while the Convention shall be, or ought to be sitting, without leave of the Convention."[311]

This rule also is duplicated in modern practice.[312] It assures that all commissioners have full notice of pending measures and time to consider them. For similar reasons, the rules of the First Continental Congress prescribed that "no question shall be determined the day, on which it is agitated and debated, if anyone of the Colonies desire the determination to be postponed to another day."[313] This prompted one

---

[308] WASHINGTON CONFERENCE REPORT, *supra* note 35, at 24.

[309] *Id.*

[310] MASON'S MANUAL, *supra* note 212, § 190.

[311] WASHINGTON CONFERENCE REPORT, *supra* note 35, at 24.

[312] MASON'S MANUAL, *supra* note 212, § 628-1.

[313] 1 JOURNALS OF THE CONTINENTAL CONGRESS 1774–1789, at 26 (Worthington Chauncey Ford et al. eds. 1904).

experienced state lawmaker to recommend a requirement of at least a day's lapse between committee approval of a measure and action by the full house. *Mason's Manual* states, "It is the usual procedure not to consider bills reported by committees when the report is received by the house, but to order the bill to second reading."[314] Because this reference seems inapplicable to conventions (which do not consider bills nor customarily provide for "readings") a day's delay between committee report and house vote may serve the purpose better.

---

[314] MASON'S MANUAL, *supra* note 212, § 670-5.

Part IV.
Forms

§ 4.1. Citizens for Self-Governance Form Application

Application for a Convention of the States under Article V of the U.S. Constitution

Whereas, the Founders of our Constitution empowered State Legislators to be guardians of liberty against future abuses of power by the federal government, and

Whereas, the federal government has created a crushing national debt through improper and imprudent spending, and

Whereas, the federal government has invaded the legitimate roles of the states through the manipulative process of federal mandates, most of which are unfunded to a great extent, and

Whereas, the federal government has ceased to live under a proper interpretation of the Constitution of the United States, and

Whereas, it is the solemn duty of the States to protect the liberty of our people—particularly for the generations to come, to propose Amendments to the Constitution of the United States through a Convention of the States under Article V to place clear restraints on these and related abuses of power,

Be it therefore resolved by the legislature of the State of _____:

Section 1. The legislature of the State of _____ hereby applies to Congress, under the provisions of Article V of the Constitution of the United States, for the calling of a convention of the states limited to proposing amendments to the Constitution of the United States that impose fiscal restraints on the federal government, limit the power and jurisdiction of the federal government, and limit the terms of office for its officials and for Members of Congress.

Section 2. The Secretary of State is hereby directed to transmit copies of this application to the President and Secretary of the United States Senate and to the Speaker and Clerk of the United States House of Representatives, and copies to the members of the said Senate and House of Representatives from this State; also to transmit copies hereof to the presiding officers of each of the legislative houses in the several States, requesting their cooperation.

Section 3. This application constitutes a continuing application in accordance with Article V of the Constitution of the United States until the legislatures of at least two thirds of the several states have made applications on the same subject.

§ 4.2. Sample Form Electing Commissioners

Resolution Electing Commissioners to Convention to Propose Amendments Restraining the Abuse of Power by the Federal Government

Whereas, the legislature of the State of _____ has applied to Congress under Article V of the United States Constitution for a convention for proposing amendments to the Constitution limited to proposing amendments that impose fiscal restraints on the federal government, limit the power and jurisdiction of the federal government, and limit the terms of office for its officials; and

Whereas, the legislature has decided to select its commissioners to the convention, if such is held:

Be it resolved by the legislature of the State of
_____,

Section 1. (commissioner 1), (commissioner 2), (commissioner 3), (commissioner 4), and (commissioner 5) are hereby elected commissioners from this state to such convention, with power to confer with commissioners from other states on the sole and exclusive subject of whether the convention shall propose amendments to the United States Constitution that impose fiscal restraints on the federal government, limit the power and jurisdiction of the federal government, and limit the terms of office for its officials and for Members of Congress, and, if so, what the terms of such amendments shall be; and further, by the decision of a majority of the commissioners from this state, to cast this state's vote in such convention.

Section 2. Unless extended by the legislature of the State of _____, the authority of such commissioners shall expire at the earlier of (1) December 31, 20__ or (2) upon any addition to the convention agenda or convention floor consideration of potential amendments or other constitutional changes other than amendments as aforesaid.

§ 4.3. Sample Commissions

Commissions are the documents appointing commissioners to represent the state legislature at a convention for proposing amendments. Below is an example of a commission issued by the State of New Jersey to five commissioners to the 1787 Constitutional Convention. One of the listed individuals, John Neilson, did not serve:

The State Of New Jersey.

To the Honorable David Brearly, William Churchill Houston, William Patterson and John Neilson Esquires. Greeting.

The Council and Assembly reposing especial trust and confidence in your integrity, prudence and ability, have at a joint meeting appointed you the said David Brearley, William Churchill

Houston, William Patterson and John Neilson Esquires, or any three of you, Commissioners to meet such Commissioners, as have been or may be appointed by the other States in the Union, at the City of Philadelphia in the Commonwealth of Pensylvania [sic], on the second Monday in May next for the purpose of taking into Consideration the state of the Union, as to trade and other important objects, and of devising such other Provisions as shall appear to be necessary to render the Constitution of the Federal Government adequate to the exigencies thereof.

In testimony whereof the Great Seal of the State is hereunto affixed. Witness William Livingston Esquire, Governor, Captain General and Commander in Chief in and over the State of New Jersey and Territories thereunto belonging Chancellor and Ordinary in the same, at Trenton the Twenty third day of November in the Year of our Lord One thousand seven hundred and Eighty six and of our Sovereignty and Independence the Eleventh.

Wil: Livingston.
By His Excellency's Command
Bowes Reed Secy.

Some modern changes:

- The state legislature rather than the state itself is the represented party at a convention for proposing amendments. This suggests that the presiding officers of each house of the state legislature ought to issue the commission.

- The commission should be tailored to the purpose of the convention, and of course modern language should be employed. The following is a possible modification:

The State Of New Jersey.
To John Jones. Greeting.

The Senate and General Assembly reposing especial trust and confidence in your integrity, prudence and ability, have at a joint meeting appointed you, Jane Doe, and Prudence Watley, Commissioners to meet such Commissioners as have been or may be appointed by the other States in the Union, in convention at the City of Denver in the State of Colorado, on May 17, 20___, pursuant to Article V of the Constitution of the United States, for the sole purpose of considering whether to propose, and if so, to draft, amendments to the United States Constitution that impose fiscal restraints on the federal government, limit the power and jurisdiction of the federal government, and limit the terms of office for its officials.

In testimony whereof the Great Seal of the State is hereunto affixed.

Witness: Frankly F. Fineagle, President of the Senate, and Georgia G. Gripper, Speaker of the Assembly, at Trenton, on the ___ day of November, 20___.

_____	_____
Speaker	President of the Senate

§ 4.4. Sample Instructions

Instructions for previous multi-state conventions were usually secret, and are difficult to recover. Some of them apparently were rambling documents, providing general guidance rather than specific rules.

The following instructions were issued by the Massachusetts legislature in 1779 as instructions for the 1780 Philadelphia Price Convention, a meeting designed to cope with continental inflation. As one can see, the commissioners were Samuel Osgood (later U.S. Postmaster General) and Elbridge Gerry (later governor of Massachusetts and Vice President of the United States). Gerry served as a commissioner to the Constitutional Convention as well. The instructions are found in volume 21 of the Acts and Resolves of the Province of Massachusetts Bay. They do not reveal much confidence in the viability of wage and price controls.

VOTE INSTRUCTING ELBRIDGE GERRY AND SAMUEL OSGOOD, ESQUIRES, COMMISSIONERS TO THE CONVENTION AT PHILADELPHIA IN JANUARY NEXT TO CONSIDER THE LIMITING OF PRICES OF PRODUCE AND MERCHANDIZE.

To the Hon. Elbridge Gerry, Esq., and Samuel Osgood, Esq.

GENTLEMEN,

The General Assembly having appointed you Commissioners to represent this State at the Convention to be held at Philadelphia, on the 1st Wednesday of January next; you are hereby authorized and impowered to meet at the time and place before mentioned such Commissioners as may be appointed by other United States, and to confer and consult with them upon the expediency of limiting the prices of articles of produce and merchandize.

In your deliberations upon this important subject, you will duly consider on the one side the advantages that it has been suggested will accrue from such a measure among others, that it will tend to give stability to our currency, prevent that inequality and injustice in private dealings, as well as in furnishing the public supplies from the several States, which have arisen from the fluctating [sic] state of prices, and that it will render it practicable for Congress and the several States to make the proper estimates for their future expences, and to fix adequate salaries upon those who are in the public service; these are important objects, and ought to be attended to. On the other side, you will duly advert to the many objections that have been made to such a plan, and the many difficulties that will attend the execution of it; for in case such a measure should be attempted and fail in the execution, you must be sensible it will be attended with many pernicious consequences, it will greatly weaken the bonds of government, as well as throw us into the greatest embarrassment, and will have a fatal tendency further to depreciate our currency. Among many other objections and difficulties that might be mentioned, and which will naturally occur to your minds in the discussion of this subject, it may be well to consider whether it has not been found that a limitation of prices, instead of appreciating or giving stability to our money has not rendered it in a manner useless, has not shut up our granaries, discouraged husbandry and commerce, and starved our Sea-Ports, in short, whether it has not created such a stagnation of business and such a witholding of articles as has obliged the people to give up the measure or submit to starving: Whether from these repeated trials and failures, that confidence, (which is so absolutely necessary in case of a limitation) is not so far lost between the States and the members of each State that this alone must prevent the execution of such a measure, as each person will be waiting to see his neighbours [sic] compliance, in the mean time witholding [sic] every supply from his friend and his country; whether it has not thrown the honest and conscientious part of the community into the hands of Sharpers, Monopolizers and Extortioners, and while it has operated as a restraint upon the former to their great loss and damage, it has not afforded an opportunity to the latter, whose only principle is that of Gain, by their cunning and deceit to aggrandize and enrich themselves, to the no small detriment of their Country.

You will also consider whether it is possible to carry an act for this purpose into execution in the method prescribed by Congress, when upon trial, it will be found, that by the method they propose the prices of labour and produce will be reduced more than two-thirds, while the articles of foreign produce will be reduced but a trifle, if any thing at all; can it be supposed the people in general will submit to it? For however reasonable it may appear to men of candour and discernment, and those who will thoroughly examine into the causes of it, yet the bulk of the people will apprehend they are imposed upon, and it will be extreamly [sic] difficult, if possible, to convince them to the contrary: You will further consider whether if such a limitation should take place, and could be effectually carried into execution, it would not be the means of disappointing Congress of such supplies of money as they depend upon from the late recommendations for taxation, and thereby oblige them to that measure which they are so very solicitous to avoid, viz. the making further emissions to defray the public expences; for is it to be supposed that the people in general would submit to such a large reduction of the prices of their produce, and at the same time submit to such large taxes as the requisitions from Congress now demand? We trust you will give these objections, as well as every thing else that may be offered pro and con upon this interesting matter in convention, their due weight, and after all, we leave it with you to act according to your best judgment and discretion, and in case you should, after mature and thorough consideration judge the measure to be expedient and practicable, and find that it is highly probable it will be adopted by all the rest of the United States, you will then proceed upon the business and make report of your proceedings to this Court, that they may take such order thereupon, as they shall then judge will best promote the public weal.

§ 4.5. The Uniform Interstate Convention Act

Commentators have proposed state enactment of legislation designed to dispel fears that a convention for proposing amendments could exceed the scope of its authority. In 2011, Michael Stern and I prepared a draft model law for state legislatures to consider. The model law is set forth below, along with its footnoted annotations. The term "delegate" has been changed to the more precise "commissioner" throughout.

This model law is designed for all interstate conventions, including but not limited to those held under Article V. Any portions not applicable to Article V (because the legislative authority of the state may not control the amendment process) may be adhered to voluntarily by the state legislature when exercising its Article V functions.

PART IV - FORMS   113

Uniform Interstate Convention Act
(Annotations in Footnotes)

Section 1. Definitions.

   (a) "Application" means an application for a convention for proposing amendments relied upon by Congress in calling such a convention.

   (b) "Commission" means the document or documents whereby the state, state legislature, or duly authorized officer of the state empowers a commissioner to an interstate convention and fixes the scope of his or her authority.[315]

   (c) "Committee" means a delegation of persons commissioned to an interstate convention.[316]

   (d) "Convention for proposing amendments"[317] means an interstate convention consisting of committees commissioned by the legislatures of the several states and called by Congress on the application of at least two thirds of such legislatures under the authority of Article V of the United States Constitution.

   (e) "Instructions" means directions given to commissioners by the commissioning authority or by that authority's agent designated for that purpose. Instructions are given contemporaneously with or subsequent to a commission, and may be amended before or during an interstate convention.[318]

---

[315] This term is taken from previous interstate convention practice.
[316] This term is taken from previous interstate convention practice.
[317] This is the official name given in Article V of the Constitution.
[318] This also follows previous convention practice.

(f) "Interstate convention" means a diplomatic meeting,[319] however denominated, of delegations ("committees") from three or more states or state legislatures[320] to consult upon and propose or adopt measures pertaining to one or more issues previously prescribed by applications, by the convention call, or by the commissioning authority.[321]

Section 2. Statements of understanding.

(a) In the years since the Declaration of Independence, and both before and after ratification of the United States Constitution, the states and state legislatures have from time to time met in interstate conventions (however denominated) to consult upon and propose or adopt measures to address prescribed problems.[322] This continued a pre-Independence practice of American colonies meeting in inter-colonial conventions and congresses.[323]

(b) The United States Constitution implicitly recognizes the authority of states and state legislatures to commission commissioners to interstate conventions, subject to the

---

[319] Interstate conventions were modeled on meetings of international diplomats. *See* RUSSELL CAPLAN, CONSTITUTIONAL BRINKSMANSHIP: AMENDING THE CONSTITUTION BY NATIONAL CONVENTION 95–96 (1988).

[320] The smallest interstate convention ever held was the Boston Convention (1780) a meeting of three states. The 1785 two-state Maryland-Virginia negotiation at Mt. Vernon pertaining to the Potomac River apparently was not considered a convention.

[321] The scope of this Uniform Law includes conventions for proposing amendments but is not limited to them. This is partly to clarify through standardization and partly to reassure people that delegates to conventions and conferences outside Article V (such as the Conference of the States proposed in 1990) are subject to instructions from "back home."

[322] *List of Conventions of States and Colonies in American History*, http://articlevinfocenter.com/list-conventions-states-colonies-american-history/.

[323] For example the Albany Congress (1754) and the First Continental Congress (1774) (also called a "convention").

limitations set forth in the Constitution. It does so implicitly in Article I, Section 10 (recognizing to interstate compacts, subject to congressional approval), explicitly though Article V (authorizing conventions for proposing amendments), and by reserving this previously-existing state power to the states through the Tenth Amendment.

(c) Although the authority to meet in convention is generally a power reserved to the states by the Constitution, in the case of a convention for proposing amendments the power is granted to the several state legislatures through the Article V of the Constitution.[324]

(d) Leading American Founders, among them James Madison, recognized the authority of states to coordinate their efforts in ways that necessarily or properly included interstate conventions.[325]

Section 3. Purposes. The purposes of this Act are

(a) to clarify the scope of authority of commissioners and committees representing this state [commonwealth] or the legislature of this state [commonwealth] at interstate conventions;

(b) to provide for enforcing limits on such authority;

(c) to provide methods of selecting and replacing commissioners to conventions; and

(d) to prescribe an oath to be taken by interstate convention commissioners.

Section 4. Number, selection, and removal of commissioners.

---

[324] On the last clause, see *United States v. Sprague*, 282 U.S. 716, 733 (1931), *Hawke v. Smith*, 253 U.S. 221 (1920), and *Dyer v. Blair*, 390 F. Supp. 1291, 1308 (N.D. Ill. 1975) (Stevens, J.) ("[T]he delegation [from Article V] is not to the states but rather to the designated ratifying bodies. . . .").

[325] *See, e.g.*, THE FEDERALIST NO. 46 (James Madison).

(a) Commissioners to a convention for proposing amendments shall be selected by a majority vote of a joint session of the legislature [or, in Nebraska "by a majority vote of the legislature].[326] Unless a different number is prescribed by the same [joint] session, the number of commissioners in this state's committee shall be three [five].[327]

(b) Commissioners to a convention for proposing amendments may be recalled and removed at any time and for any reason by a majority vote of a [joint] session of the legislature, and, if the legislature is not in session, may be suspended pending such a vote by a [joint] legislative committee duly authorized by the legislature for that purpose.

(c) The number and methods of selection and removal of commissioners to other conventions shall be as prescribed by law.[328]

Section 5. Vacancies.

(a) Vacancies in committees representing the state legislature at a convention for proposing amendments shall be filled by the [joint] legislative committee duly authorized for that purpose until such time as a vote by [a joint session of] the legislature shall select a permanent replacement.

(b) Vacancies in committees of commissioners at other interstate conventions shall be filled as prescribed by law

---

[326] Nebraska's legislature is unicameral. Bracketed language hereinafter should be deleted in Nebraska.

[327] The legislature should choose an odd number so the state committee will not be deadlocked in state-by-state voting. State committees at the 1787 Constitutional Convention ranged from two commissioners (New Hampshire) to eight (Pennsylvania).

[328] This is left flexible so it may vary according the nature and importance of the convention.

or, in absence of governing law, by the authority commissioning the commissioners.

Section 6. Limitations on commissioners' powers.

(a) No commissioner shall exceed the scope of authority granted by his or her commission or violate his or her instructions.

(b) In the case of a convention for proposing amendments, the scope of authority granted by any commission and instructions shall not be deemed to exceed the narrowest of

(i) the scope of the congressional call,

(ii) the scope of the narrowest application among those cited by Congress as mandating the convention call, or

(iii) the actual terms of the commission and instructions.[329]

Section 7. Oath.

(a) Prior to or contemporaneously with receiving his or her commission, each commissioner shall take the following oath: "I do solemnly swear (or affirm) that I accept and will act according to the limits of authority specified in my commission, by any present or subsequent instructions, and by the Uniform Interstate Convention Act. I understand that violating this oath may subject me to penalties provided by law."

(b) No person shall serve as a commissioner prior to taking the oath specified in subsection (a).

Section 8. Offense of exceeding scope of authority at an interstate convention.

---

[329] This is kept narrow so that the commissioners do not exceed the scope of the convention as agreed to by all applying states. It is unfair to impose a broader call upon a state that agreed in its application only to a narrower call.

(a) A person commits the offense of exceeding the scope of authority at an interstate convention if, while serving as a commissioner at an interstate convention, he or she votes for, votes to consider, or otherwise promotes any action of the convention not within the scope defined in Section 6; provided, however, that a commissioner may vote for or otherwise support a measure clearly identified as a non-binding recommendation rather than as a formal proposal.[330]

(b) A person committing the offense of exceeding the scope of authority at an interstate convention shall be subject to the same punishments applicable to a person convicted of perjury.[331]

§ 4.6. Historic Examples of Multi-State Convention Calls[332]

The following five calls are fairly typical of the breed, so to speak. Three were issued during the Founding Era, one in 1861, and one in 2017.

Congressional Call to the York Town & Charleston Price Conventions (1777)[333]

That, for this purpose, it be recommended to the legislatures, or, in their recess, to the executive powers of the States of New York, New Jersey, Pensylvania [sic], Delaware, Maryland, and

---

[330] Issuing non-binding recommendations—clearly denominated as such—is a universally recognized prerogative of American conventions, adopted, for example, by seven of the state conventions that ratified the Constitution and by the Annapolis Convention of 1786.

[331] The perjury benchmark is selected because of the oath. States may apply other benchmarks, and where there are degrees of a crime, must select a degree.

[332] Natelson, *Conventions, supra* note 2, at 668–70 includes details from the calls for numerous other conventions as well.

[333] For more information on the abortive York Town and Charleston Price Conventions, see *id.*, at 644–47.

Virginia, to appoint commissioners to meet at York town, in Pensylvania, on the 3d Monday in March next, to consider of, and form a system of regulation adapted to those States, to be laid before the respective legislatures of each State, for their approbation:

That, for the like purpose, it be recommended to the legislatures, or executive powers in the recess of the legislatures of the States of North Carolina, South Carolina, and Georgia, to appoint commissioners to meet at Charlestown [sic], in South Carolina, on the first Monday in May next. . . .[334]

Massachusetts' Call to the Springfield Convention (1777)[335]

The General Assembly of this state, taking into their consideration the state of the bills of credit emitted by this and the neighboring governments, and finding the measures that have already been adopted . . . have not effectually answered the purpose of supporting the credit of said bills . . . have chosen a committee to meet such committees, as may be appointed by the states of New Hampshire, Rhode Island, Connecticut and New York, on the 30th day of July next, at the town of Springfield, in the county of Hampshire, within this state, to confer together upon this interesting subject, and consider what steps can be taken effectually to support the credit of the public currencies, and prevent their being counterfeited; and to confer upon such other matters as are particularly mentioned in the resolve enclosed. . . .[336]

---

[334] 7 JOURNALS OF THE CONTINENTAL CONGRESS 1774–1789, at 124 (Worthington Chauncey Ford et al. eds., 1907)

[335] For more information on the Springfield Convention of 1787, see Natelson, *Conventions, supra* note 2, at 647–49.

[336] 1 THE PUBLIC RECORDS OF THE STATE OF CONNECTICUT 599 (Charles J. Hoodly ed., 1894) (reproducing Massachusetts resolution).

Virginia's Combined Call and Authorization of Commissioners for the Constitutional Convention (1787)[337]

Whereas the Commissioners who assembled at Annapolis on the fourteenth day of September last for the purpose of devising and reporting the means of enabling Congress to provide effectually for the Commercial Interests of the United States have represented the necessity of extending the revision of the foederal System to all it's [cgf] defects and have recommended that Deputies for that purpose be appointed by the several Legislatures to meet in Convention in the City of Philadelphia on the second day of May next a provision which was preferable to a discussion of the subject in Congress . . .

Be It Therefore Enacted by the General Assembly of the Commonwealth of Virginia that seven Commissioners be appointed by joint Ballot of both Houses of Assembly who or any three of them are hereby authorized as Deputies from this Commonwealth to meet such Deputies as may be appointed and authorized by other States to assemble in Convention at Philadelphia as above recommended and to join with them in devising and discussing all such Alterations and farther Provisions as may be necessary to render the Foederal Constitution adequate to the Exigencies of the Union and in reporting such an Act for that purpose to the United States in Congress as when agreed to by them and duly confirmed by the several States will effectually provide for the same. And Be It Further Enacted that in case of the death of any of the said Deputies or of their declining their appointments the Executive are hereby authorized to supply such Vacancies. And the

---

[337] Virginia issued the call for the Constitutional Convention on December 1, 1786 in response to the recommendation of the Annapolis Convention. For more information about the call for the Constitutional Convention, see Natelson, *Conventions, supra* note 2, at 674–80 and Michael Farris, *Defying Conventional Wisdom: The Constitution Was Not the Product of a Runaway Convention*, 40 HARVARD J. L. & PUB. POL'Y 61 (2017). To view the credentials issued by the states to their delegates for the Constitutional Convention, see 3 FARRAND'S RECORDS, *supra* note 48, at 559–86.

Governor is requested to transmit forthwith a Copy of this Act to the United States in Congress and to the Executives of each of the States in the Union.[338]

Virginia's Call to Washington Conference Convention (1861)[339]

Resolved, That on behalf of the commonweath [sic] of Virginia, an invitation is hereby extended to all such States, whether slaveholding or non-slaveholding, as are willing to unite with Virginia in an earnest effort to adjust the present unhappy controversies, in the spirit in which the Constitution was originally formed, and consistently with its principles, so as to afford to the people of the slaveholding States adequate guarantees for the security of their rights, to appoint commissioners to meet on the fourth day of February next, in the City of Washington, similar commisioners [sic] appointed by Virginia, to consider, and if practicable, agree upon some suitable adjustment.[340]

Arizona's Call to the Balanced Budget Amendment Planning Convention (2017)

This call, while deferential to the discretion of the participating states, included recommendations (not reproduced here) added because of the widespread modern unfamiliarity with the convention of states process.[341] The operative language of the call is as follows:

. . . [The State of Arizona respectfully calls a planning convention of the states, consisting of commissioners chosen and authorized in the manner that each respective state legislature determines or, if no manner is determined by a state legislature, selected jointly by the majority leadership of each legislative chamber of that state, to convene initially at twelve o'clock noon on

---

[338] 3 FARRAND'S RECORDS, *supra* note 48, 559–63.

[339] For more information on the Washington Conference Convention, see *supra* note 35 and accompanying text, and *infra* § 3.14.2–.5.

[340] WASHINGTON CONFERENCE REPORT, *supra* note 35, at 9.

[341] Ariz. House Concurrent Resolution 2022, *available at* https://www.azleg.gov/legtext/53leg/1R/laws/hcr2022.pdf.

September 12, 2017 in Phoenix, Arizona for the limited purposes of:

(a) Planning for, and recommending rules for and procedures to, the prospective convention for proposing a balanced budget amendment to the United States Constitution.

(b) Recommending to Congress:

(i) The criteria for determining the initial date and location of a convention for proposing a balanced budget amendment.

(ii) A specific initial date and location of a convention for proposing a balanced budget amendment.

That the planning convention shall be called to order jointly by the Speaker of the House of Representatives and the President of the Senate of the State of Arizona, followed immediately by a roll call of the states. The planning convention shall immediately elect a permanent presiding officer by a majority vote of the states attending and voting under the parliamentary common law as modified by procedures traditionally followed by conventions of states, including the rule of one vote per state. The planning convention shall continue to operate under the traditional procedures until such time as the planning convention adopts its own rules.

That the Legislature of the State of Arizona recognizes that a convention of states determines its own rules and procedures and elects its own officers. In the interests of efficiency and consistency, however, the Legislature of the State of Arizona recommends to the planning convention that the permanent rules contain certain principles traditionally followed by conventions of states, including the following [recommendations follow].

§ 4.7. Model Convention Rules

An earlier draft of these rules was prepared for the Simulated Convention of States held in Williamsburg, Virginia in 2016. They were based heavily on historical practice, modified for modern conditions on the advice of several experienced state lawmakers, one of whom had served in legislative leadership in two states.

The experience at Williamsburg fully justified reliance on historical practice, as modified: They worked almost flawlessly. The experience of the Williamsburg simulation did suggest a few modifications, which have been incorporated. Rules 17 and 18 (providing for committees) assume the convention is authorized to propose within the subject areas covered by the three-topic "Convention of States" application pending before the state legislatures as of the date of publication of this treatise. Conventions considering other subjects should amend Rule 17 accordingly and either omit or refine Rule 18.

Convention for Proposing Amendments—Proposed Rules

Rule 1. Source of Default Rules
Rule 2. Members of the Convention
Rule 3. Voting
Rule 4. Officers
Rule 5. Number of Commissioners on the Floor
Rule 6. Quorum
Rule 7. Order of Business
Rule 8. Decorum in Debate
Rule 9. Selection of Speaker
Rule 10. Limits on Speaking
Rule 11. Motions
Rule 12. Division of Questions
Rule 13. Deferral of Vote
Rule 14. Questions of Order
Rule 15. Absence
Rule 16. Costs.
Rule 17. Committees—Generally Applicable Provisions
Rule 18. Fiscal Restraints, Federal Jurisdiction, and Term Limits Committees

*****

Rule 1. <u>Source of Default Rules</u>. Questions not governed by these rules shall be governed by the latest published edition of

Mason's Manual of Legislative Procedure,[342] except where the rule in that manual can be applied only to a state legislature rather than a convention, in which case the matter shall be determined by parliamentary common law.[343]

Rule 2. Members of the Convention. The members of this convention are the committees (hereinafter called *delegations*)[344] appointed by their respective states.[345]

Rule 3. Voting

(a) All votes on the floor of the convention and in the committee of the whole shall be taken by states, with each state having one vote.[346]

(b) Each state delegation's vote shall be determined in accordance with the rule prescribed by the commissioning state.[347] Every delegation shall canvass each

---

[342] Seventy of the ninety-nine state legislative chambers currently use *Mason's Manual* as their source of default rules. Additional reasons for selecting this source are explained *supra* § 3.14.4. The 1850 Nashville convention designated Jefferson's rules for the U.S. Senate as a default source, but they are more dated and less familiar to most state lawmakers than *Mason's*.

[343] The parliamentary common law is the American common law of organizational procedures built up over several centuries. It is so named because it originated from procedures in the British Parliament. *See* MASON'S MANUAL, *supra* note 212, § 35. *See also supra* § 3.14.

[344] "Committee" was the traditional designation of a delegation to an interstate convention. These rules use "delegation" to avoid confusion with convention committees.

[345] This is a clarification of precedent and of sometimes-confusing earlier convention rules.

[346] Voting within committees other than the committee of the whole is per capita—that is, by person. When it is important that intra-committee votes be weighed by states, the committee may consist of one commissioner from each state, also voting per capita. (See Rule 18.) These procedures generally follow former practice.

[347] This is called an "internal quorum rule." For example, in a delegation of five, the internal quorum rule may provide that the state may cast a vote

commissioner on each vote in a manner to be prescribed by the commissioning state or, in default of a prescribed manner, by the delegation.

(c) On roll call votes, states shall declare their votes in alphabetical order,[348] with each state's vote announced by a single person designated by that delegation.

(d) On every voice vote, each delegation's vote shall be called only a single person designated by that delegation.[349] A call for a division after a voice vote shall be considered a call for a roll call vote.

Rule 4. <u>Officers</u>

(a) A temporary convention president shall be appointed from among the commissioners from the state that was the first to enact the application leading to the convention call and still in effect when the convention was called. The temporary president shall be selected by a majority vote of that state's delegation. The temporary president's sole duty shall be to preside over the election of the convention president, and he or she shall be ineligible to be the permanent president.

(b) The permanent officers of the convention shall consist of a president and vice president, who shall be elected from among the commissioners; and the following, who shall be elected from among persons not commissioners: secre-

---

only if a majority of at least three commissioners are present and voting. Or the state could require that all commissioners in the delegation be present and voting and that at least four vote one way. Or it could provide that if only one commissioner from that state is present, then he or she may cast the state's vote. This is a matter for each state legislature to determine.

[348] The traditional order was for states to vote from northeast to southwest, but the current configuration of the country makes that difficult, and the alphabetical system is more familiar to modern Americans.

[349] Earlier drafts had the announcement made by the delegation chairman. However, that presents problems if that person is not present or has a weak voice. This version gives each delegation more flexibility.

tary, sergeant-at-arms, parliamentarian, and assistant parliamentarian.[350]

(c) Election as an officer shall be by a majority vote of states present and voting. In the event that no candidate receives a majority in the first round of voting, there shall be successive voting rounds until a candidate wins a majority. On successive voting rounds, those candidates shall be dropped who received the fewest votes on the preceding round and whose vote totals amount to the lowest number sufficient that, if cast for the leader in the preceding round, would have given him or her a majority.[351]

---

[350] This is derived from the practice of previous interstate conventions. The recommendation that there be a parliamentarian is an innovation based on a recommendation by an experienced legislator. *Supra* § 3.14.3. Some conventions have appointed assistant secretaries, but it would seem better to allow the secretary to appoint assistants who are not necessarily commissioners.

[351] The requirement of a majority rather than a plurality assures that officers have wide bases of support. Here is an example of how the elimination rule works:

Assume 50 states are present and voting. In that event, 26 is a majority.
On the **first ballot** the tally is:
Candidate A: 20 votes
Candidate B: 15 votes
Candidate C: 9 votes
Candidate D: 3 votes
Candidate E: 3 votes
At this point, Candidates D and E should be dropped because theirs is the lowest combined vote total (6) that if cast for Candidate A would give Candidate A a majority.
Second Ballot:
Candidate A: 23 votes
Candidate B: 17 votes
Candidate C: 10 votes.
At this point, Candidate C should be cut and the final runoff held between A and B.

(d) Each convention officer shall discharge the duties of such officer pursuant to *Mason's Manual* and parliamentary common law, subject to alteration by the convention. All officers shall be on oath to carry out their duties faithfully and in accordance with lawful authority.

(e) The secretary shall prepare and provide to each commissioner at the opening of beginning of business on each day a calendar or agenda of business scheduled for that day.

(f) Each delegation shall file its internal quorum rules[352] with the secretary. In the event of a challenge to a state vote because of claimed violation of that state's internal quorum rules, the secretary shall advise the chair as to whether the internal quorum rules were complied with.

(g) The sergeant-at-arms is empowered, under direction of the presiding officer,[353] to secure the good order of the house. Orders issued by the presiding officer to the sergeant-of-arms shall be appealable, as in the case of other rulings of the chair.[354]

Rule 5. <u>Number of Commissioners on the Floor</u>. Irrespective of how many commissioners a state includes within its delegation,

---

[352] *Accord*: Convention Resolution 1, Recommended Rules § 3.2.1, in JOURNAL, *supra* note 11 (unpaginated, but on sheet 276). A state's internal quorum rule is the rule by which a state committee (delegation) casts that state's vote. It is determined by the state legislature sending the delegation or by its delegatee. (See Rule 3 and accompanying note.) Whatever rule the state decides on, it must be filed with the secretary, who will have to familiarize himself with each one.

[353] The term "presiding officer" is used throughout these rules rather than "president" because there may be times when the president is absent and the gavel taken up by the vice president or another substitute.

[354] This rule follows the parliamentary common law, see *supra* § 3.14.1, but is placed here to answer questions about how the convention will control internal demonstrations or disorder.

no more than [three] [five] commissioners from any one state shall be on the floor at the same time.[355]

Rule 6. <u>Quorum</u>. A quorum to do business shall consist of the commissioners empowered to cast the votes of more than half of the state delegations accredited to the convention,[356] and all questions shall be decided by the greater number of delegations

---

[355]This rule does *not* limit the size of any state's delegation. Determining the size of the delegation is wholly the prerogative of the state legislature sending it. However, placing a maximum number of commissioners on the floor from any one state at any one time cures the unfair and potentially unruly situation arising at the 1850 Nashville Convention, where Tennessee, although having only one vote, sent 100 commissioners—more than all other states combined.

Interstate conventions originated as diplomatic negotiations. As the number of states increased, their dynamics more closely resembled a deliberative legislative body. Both models worked well. However, increasing size beyond a certain level could convert a convention into a large assembly without significant deliberation and into mere ratifying body for decisions made by a select group.

This rule gives the convention the option of an on-the-floor maximum of either three or five. The choice of three would create an assembly of no more than 150; the choice of five a maximum of 250. Arguing for five is that five is within the historical range of delegation size. Arguing for three is the affirmative experience of the Washington Convention and Williamsburg simulations, which demonstrated that an assembly of 130-150 participants worked very well, and the negative experience of Nashville, which showed that than 150 could become unwieldy.

The choice of the maximum floor number is for the convention to make. It will want to make that choice based on several considerations, including state preferences, political factors, available technology, and physical factors.

[356] An earlier draft fixed the quorum at 26 delegations, i.e., a majority of all states. It has been changed to a majority of delegations accredited to the convention in order to prevent states that refuse to attend from preventing a quorum and thereby blocking the work of the convention.

present and voting; but in absence of a quorum a majority of delegations present and voting may adjourn from day to day.[357]

Rule 7. <u>Order of Business</u>. The order of business shall be as follows:[358]

    (1) call to order,

    (2) roll call of the states, and Secretary's announcement of a quorum present,

    (3) invocation,

    (4) pledge of allegiance,

    (5) reading and approval by the clerk of the minutes of the previous day,

    (6) reports of standing committees,

    (7) reports of special or select committees,

    (8) special orders,

    (9) unfinished business,

    (10) introduction and first reading of proposals,

    (11) consideration of daily calendar,

    (12) announcement of committee meetings, and

    (13) recess for the day (adjournment).

Rule 8. <u>Decorum in Debate</u>.

    (a) Every commissioner rising to speak shall address the presiding officer, and while he or she shall is speaking no one shall pass between them or read any

---

[357] This is based, with an adjustment for the larger number of states, on the rules of the 1861 Washington Convention. See *supra* § 3.14.3.

[358] This is the order in *Mason's Manual*, as modified for a convention. *Supra* § 3.14.5. The pledge of allegiance has been added.

written matter not immediately germane to the question under consideration.[359]

(b) A commissioner may be called to order by another commissioner, as well as by the presiding officer, and shall be allowed to explain his or her conduct or any expressions supposed to be reprehensible.[360]

Rule 9. Selection of Speaker. Of two commissioners rising to speak at the same time, the presiding officer shall name the one who shall first be heard.[361]

Rule 10. Limits on Speaking.

(a) A commissioner shall not speak more often than twice without special leave upon the same question, and not a second time before every other who had been silent but chooses to speak on the subject shall have been heard. The commissioners from any one delegation shall not speak more often than five times without special leave upon the same question, and not more than three times before every other who had been silent but chooses to speak on the subject has been heard.[362]

(b) No commissioner shall, without leave of the convention, speak more than 10 minutes at any one time.[363]

Rule 11. Motions.

(a) Each motion shall require a second from a delegation other than the delegation of the movant.[364]

---

[359] This is based on the rules prevailing both at the 1787 Philadelphia Convention and the 1861 Washington Convention, although modified to take account of modern technology. *Supra* § 3.14.5.

[360] *Supra* § 3.14.5.

[361] *Id.*

[362] *Id.* The last sentence of this rule was added to prevent filibusters by large state delegations, which might otherwise rotate their commissioners on and off the floor so as to dominate debate.

[363] Added to reflect modern conditions, *supra* § 3.14.5.

(b) Once seconded, each motion shall be repeated; and if written, as it shall be when any commissioner shall so require, shall be read aloud by the secretary and, before it shall be debated, shall be either placed on a common screen or transmitted to each commissioner's pre-designated electronic device.[365]

(c) No motion, other than a procedural motion, shall be in order unless within the scope of both the subject matter specified in the state applications on which Congress called the convention and of the subject matter specified in the convention call.[366]

(d) A call for the previous question is a suggestion that debate be terminated. A motion to structure debate is a motion to adopt a limit on debate for the matter on the floor. A motion for the previous question is a motion to close

---

[364] MASON'S MANUAL, *supra* note 212, at §§ 62 & 157, dispenses with seconds, but several participants in the Williamsburg simulation suggested seconds are useful in demonstrating substantial support, especially if required from a delegation other than the delegation of the movant. Previous conventions required seconds, and successful experience is generally persuasive.

[365] Based on the Washington Convention rules, *supra*, § 3.14.5, but updated for modern conditions.

[366] This rule provides that a substantive motion is out of order unless within the scope of the subjects in the applications and call, whichever is narrower. Normally, the subject matter of the applications and the call would be the same. In some cases, however, some of the 34 applications that trigger a convention on a particular subject might mention extraneous subjects. This language makes clear that the convention is to consider only subjects on which at least 34 applications agree, and which therefore are or should be reflected in the scope of the call. An earlier draft of these rules stated that substantive motions must be "germane" to the subject matter. This draft changes that language to a requirement that they be "within the scope of" the subject matter. This is because, as sometimes applied, the standard of "germaneness" may not be sufficiently strict to assure that the convention remains within its rightful authority. The germaneness test is retained in Rules 8 and 23.

debate. The presiding officer may permit a brief closing statement by the movant after closing debate.[367]

(e) A motion to reconsider a matter that has been determined by a majority may be made, with leave unanimously given, on the same day on which the vote passed; but otherwise not without one day's previous notice; in which last case, if the convention agree to the reconsideration, the convention or, by the convention's leave, the presiding officer shall assign a future day for the purpose.[368]

(f) A motion to recess for the day may be made at any time, and if seconded the question shall be put without debate.

(g) A motion may be withdrawn at any time before the vote upon it shall have been declared.[369]

Rule 12. *Division of Questions*. A question that consists of one or more propositions shall, at the request of any commissioner, be divided and put separately as to each proposition.[370]

Rule 13. *Deferral of Vote*. No substantive question or committee recommendation shall be decided the day on which it is introduced or first debated if any five states request that the decision be postponed to another day.[371]

---

[367] The practice reflected by the last sentence has been controversial, but apparently is common among state legislatures. A closing statement is left to the ruling of the chair, which like other rulings, is appealable.

[368] Based on a rule of the 1787 Philadelphia Convention, with language updated.

[369] Based on the Washington Convention rules.

[370] Based on a rule of the Washington Convention. The language has been updated.

[371] This is loosely based on the 1774 New York City convention usually known as the First Continental Congress, but represents a compromise between the need for speed and a rule that mandated delay at the request of any delegation. *Id.*

Rule 14. <u>Questions of Order</u>. All questions of order shall be decided by the presiding officer, subject to appeal to the convention, but without debate.[372]

Rule 15. <u>Absence</u>. No commissioner shall be absent from the convention, so as to interrupt the representation of his or her state, without leave.[373]

Rule 16. <u>Costs</u>. The common costs of the convention shall be divided equally among the legislatures sending commissioners. The costs related to the travel, maintenance and provisioning of each state's delegation and staff shall be borne entirely by that state.[374]

Rule 17. <u>Committees—Generally Applicable Provisions.</u>

(a) The standing committees shall include committees on rules, credentials, administration, fiscal restraints, federal jurisdiction, and term limits.[375] The convention may create a committee of the whole and ad hoc committees.

(b) Voting within committees, other than the committee of the whole, shall be per capita.[376]

---

[372] A proposed rule of the Washington Convention would have dispensed with the right of appeal, but the delegates rejected that provision. *Supra* § 3.14.5.

[373] Based on a rule of the Washington Convention, with updated language. *Supra* § 3.14.5.

[374] This rule is patterned on that recommended by the Phoenix Planning Convention. Convention Resolution 1, Recommended Rules, § 6.1, in JOURNAL, *supra* note 11, (unpaginated but on sheet 279).

[375] The requirement for standing committees on fiscal restraints, federal jurisdiction, and term limits is based on the three-subject model application of Citizens for Self-Governance's "Convention of States" movement.

[376] The per capita rule for in-committee voting reflects previous convention practice. Where equal state representation on a committee is important, it should consist of one commissioner from each state.

(c) The procedures of the committee of the whole, including voting, shall be governed by these rules, except insofar as altered by that committee.

(d) The membership of the rules, credentials, and administration committees shall be elected by a plurality of the states, voting by secret ballot.[377] The officers of those committees and of any committee of the whole shall be selected by a majority vote of their respective committees, using the procedure for electing officers of the convention, except that in committees other than the committee of the whole voting shall be per capita rather than by state.

(e) The membership and chairmen of ad hoc committees shall be appointed by the president or other officer presiding at the time, unless the convention shall prescribe another method.

(f) The membership of the fiscal restraints, federal jurisdiction, and term limits committees shall be selected by the method designated in Rule 18.

(g) Each committee may by majority vote create subcommittees for issues germane to the committee's assigned task.

---

[377] Prior conventions have filled committees both by plurality election and presidential appointment. Here, elections are reserved for the three most important committees. The convention is free to prescribe election at any time for other committees.

Earlier convention rules refer to "ballot." The word "secret" is added because modern Americans may not be aware that the term "ballot" traditionally implies secrecy. Although most of the secrecy rules applied in older conventions have been dropped, secrecy may be necessary in this case to ensure an impartial choice and to minimize hard feelings that may impair convention efficiency.

Convention officers should have sufficiently wide support to command majority votes (Rule 4), but pluralities are better for committees because committees consist of several different persons. Moreover, election by plurality avoids run-off votes, which could be particularly time-consuming for committees.

(h) Committees and subcommittees shall not sit while the convention shall be or ought to be sitting, without leave of the convention.[378]

Rule 18. <u>Fiscal Restraints, Federal Jurisdiction, and Term Limits Committees [designed only for the three-subject "Convention of States" application]</u>.[379]

(a) The fiscal restraints committee, federal jurisdiction committee, and term limits committee each has [exclusive][380] responsibility for developing proposals within the corresponding subject matter of the state applications for the convention.

(b) Each of these three committees shall consist of one commissioner from each state delegation, and one commissioner only, selected as determined by such delegation;[381] provided however, that no person shall serve on more than one of those three committees.

---

[378] Based on a rule of the Washington Convention and modern legislative practice. *Supra* § 3.14.5.

[379] This Rule sets forth a procedure for proposals within those three subjects, and prevents presiding officers from refusing to permit debate or votes on credible proposals within those three areas.

[380] Inclusion of the term *exclusive* would prevent the convention from creating committees to "wire around" the three standing committees mentioned in this section. There are obvious advantages and disadvantages to both including and omitting the term "exclusive."

[381] This provision for one commissioner from each state on each of the three subject-matter committees is designed to ensure a free flow of proposals and protection for the interests of each state. It was adopted at the Williamsburg Simulation in 2016. Your author served as legal counsel to one of the three subject-matter committees, and in his view the committee size was unwieldy. A way to reduce the size while still preserving openness is to reduce the membership of each of these three committees to 10 or 12 with per capita voting, but to provide for plurality election (as with other committees) and that none of these three committees may have more than one member from any state.

(c) Any proposal approved by a subcommittee of any of these three committees shall be referred to its committee chairman, who shall schedule it for hearing within five days of its referral from the subcommittee. The committee shall vote on any proposal endorsed by at least five committee members within 24 hours after the hearing (weekends and holidays excluded). Approval shall be by a simple majority of committee members present and voting.

(d) Every proposal reported from the fiscal restraints, federal jurisdiction, or term limits committee shall be scheduled for debate and a vote on the floor of the convention; the presiding officer of the convention shall have no authority to refuse to schedule debate or a vote on any such proposal, and no formal rule shall be required to schedule any such proposal for debate or a vote. No motion to adjourn *sine die* shall be in order so long as any such proposal remains without a convention vote to pass, reject, or table.

Made in the USA
Lexington, KY
14 January 2019